Lumion 3D Cookbook

Revolutionize your Lumion skills with over 100 recipes
to create stunning architectural visualizations

Ciro Cardoso

BIRMINGHAM - MUMBAI

Lumion 3D Cookbook

First published: June 2014

Production Reference: 1100614

Published by Packt Publishing Ltd.
Livery Place
35 Livery Street
Birmingham B3 2PB, UK.

ISBN 978-1-78355-093-7

www.packtpub.com

Cover Image by Ciro Cardoso (cirocardoso@sapo.pt)

Credits

Author

Ciro Cardoso

Reviewers

CJ Arquitecto

Ahmed Osama El-Bakry

Gianfranco Maiorano

Commissioning Editor

Kunal Parikh

Acquisition Editor

Subho Gupta

Content Development Editor

Nadeem N. Bagban

Technical Editor

Mrunal Chavan

Copy Editors

Sarang Chari

Mradula Hegde

Gladson Monteiro

Adithi Shetty

Project Coordinator

Venitha Cutinho

Proofreaders

Maria Gould

Paul Hindle

Indexers

Tejal Soni

Priya Subramani

Production Coordinator

Sushma Redkar

Cover Work

Sushma Redkar

About the Author

Ciro Cardoso is a self-taught 3D artist and a training author from an architectural background, who started experimenting with creative software and 3D applications back in 2000. In 2005, he started his own small multimedia business, working on projects as diverse as graphic designing, CAD services, architectural visualization projects, and web designing, successfully using Lumion for multimillion-dollar projects. His list of personal clients covers countries such as the United Kingdom, Portugal, the Netherlands, Angola, and Cape Verde.

He is quite literate with software in general, with extensive expertise on Maya, 3ds Max, AutoCAD, SketchUp, Photoshop, Lumion, Unreal Development Kit, and Bentley Microstation. He is also the author of *Getting Started with Lumion 3D, Packt Publishing*.

Besides his work as a 3D artist, he also does some voluntary work teaching 3D modeling and architectural visualization with SketchUp and CAD to youngsters. He can be reached through his website at `http://www.cirocardoso.net`.

I would like to thank the Packt Publishing team for their effort and amazing, remarkable, and wonderful work to produce this book, and also for this opportunity. Also, a truthful thanks to all my reviewers for their constructive and detailed reviews.

Finally, I have to express my gratitude to my family, in particular, my wife, for her support, love, and patience. Also, a quick thanks to my mother-in-law for asking me almost every single day whether the book was ready.

About the Reviewers

CJ Arquitecto is a young Portuguese architect born in Lagos, Portugal, in June 1984. He loves architecture and likes photography, 3D modeling, and 3D rendering. He uses these skills to communicate his work and ideas around the world. He entered the world of art with the first sketch he made on his sofa at the age of one. Then, while playing with Lego and Playmobil, a cliché for any architect, he discovered that he would love to be an architect. So, he pursued his dream of becoming one. With this aim in mind, at the age of 24, he finished his degree in Architecture from the University of Porto, also known as the Faculty of Architecture of Porto, Siza Vieira. He defines the importance of photography with regards to his professional work as an intimate relationship. He projects the desire to expose his imaginary and biographical stories, adventures, and misadventures by stopping them in time through a simple click while working on his projects. Also, he has been developing several architectural projects, mostly in Africa; these include projects that range from residential houses to sports complex centers. By the time he started reviewing this book, he was working on an architectural project for Luanda and was glad to be a part of the Packt Publishing team. You can find more information about him at `archinect.com/cjarchitect`.

Ahmed Osama El-Bakry was born and brought up in Cairo; he was born on August 16, 1990. He got his BSc degree from Ain Shams University, the urban planning and design (UPD) department, in July 2012. He worked as a teaching assistant at Ain Shams University in the urban planning and design department. His accumulative ranking is the first among his colleagues. He completed his premaster studies, the duration of which was a year, from the same college that he graduated from. Then, he joined the IUSD Master's program between Stuttgart University, Germany, and Ain Shams University, Egypt. While still part of this program, he began with his practical work by participating in urban competitions such as redesigning the El Opera and El Ataba square project, the Tahrir square project, and others at Cairo. He works as an executive engineer for some interior architectural projects such as the renovation of the IUSD branch in Egypt at Ain Shams University. He also works as a freelancer for several urban and architectural projects, especially in Saudi Arabia. When he was an undergraduate, he participated in a student exchange program and had the opportunity to study at Ain Shams University; Artesis University, school of architecture, Antwerp, Belgium; and l'ecole de' Belleville, Paris, France; this happened in December 2010 and the program was about urbanism and future developments. He attended several conferences and workshops on sustainable urbanism, different and contemporary planning approaches, and development of cooperation between countries, which were organized by UN-habitat, GIZ, and BMZ at Germany. He also deals with several engineering and graphical programs, which has led him to have a part in reviewing this book.

Gianfranco Maiorano is a creative and talented architect and an EU-licensed construction engineer; he is based in London, United Kingdom, since 2013. He studied and completed his master's degree in Architecture and Construction Engineering from the University of Bologna, Italy. His experience after his graduation covers both public and private projects in the UK and Italy, including several competition submissions.

Since childhood, Gianfranco has been very passionate about architecture. He possesses a natural intellectual capacity and curiosity about his chosen field. These skills have led him to develop a keen interest in conducting research on contemporary architecture, art, and digital tools, especially in connection to quantum physics and parametric and generative techniques for architecture. He possesses exceptional technical expertise with regards to a wide range of software from 3D modeling and BIM to visualization and animation. His inspiration comes from artists such as Lucio Fontana, Antony Gormley, and Anish Kapoor, and architects such as Renzo Piano, Ben van Berkel, and Rem Koolhaas. He can be contacted on his website at www.gianfrancomaiorano.com.

www.PacktPub.com

Support files, eBooks, discount offers, and more

You might want to visit www.PacktPub.com for support files and downloads related to your book.

Did you know that Packt offers eBook versions of every book published, with PDF and ePub files available? You can upgrade to the eBook version at www.PacktPub.com and as a print book customer, you are entitled to a discount on the eBook copy. Get in touch with us at service@packtpub.com for more details.

At www.PacktPub.com, you can also read a collection of free technical articles, sign up for a range of free newsletters and receive exclusive discounts and offers on Packt books and eBooks.

http://PacktLib.PacktPub.com

Do you need instant solutions to your IT questions? PacktLib is Packt's online digital book library. Here, you can access, read and search across Packt's entire library of books.

Why subscribe?

- Fully searchable across every book published by Packt
- Copy and paste, print and bookmark content
- On demand and accessible via web browser

Free access for Packt account holders

If you have an account with Packt at www.PacktPub.com, you can use this to access PacktLib today and view nine entirely free books. Simply use your login credentials for immediate access.

Table of Contents

Preface

Welcome to *Lumion 3D Cookbook*. Lumion is a real-time render engine, and is perfect for most users as it allows them to create their content quickly and easily; this allows architectural visualizations to meet and exceed the standards of quality with fewer resources.

With this book, we will deliver the best of what Lumion has to offer and how to use Lumion's intuitive and powerful tools for bringing your visions to life.

While reading this book, you will be taken through a wide variety of topics that will help you improve your workflow and your project's quality. You will start with some basic notions that will ensure that you start a project with the right foot; also, across the book, you will find recipes that will not only help you set up a solid and well-organized project, but also increase the quality and detail of the still image or movie that you'll produce.

This is a Cookbook; this means that you will have recipes that are straight to the point and cover what you need to do to achieve a specific goal. A recipe alone will not create an astonishing render, but the combination of several recipes will unlock the true potential of *Lumion 3D Cookbook*.

What this book covers

Chapter 1, Importing in Lumion, will focus entirely on how to import your own 3D models and also provide some techniques and Lumion's tools that are essential to work with, organize, and protect your imported 3D models.

Chapter 2, Placing the Content, helps you understand what can be accomplished with Lumion's library and also all the 3D models available to populate your project.

Chapter 3, Manipulating and Controlling 3D Models, will provide you with the best techniques to select, manipulate, and modify the content placed in the Lumion's scene.

Chapter 4, Constructing Your World, provides you with the techniques to start shaping the world and make it more appealing. How to merge parts of your 3D model seamlessly with the terrain and how to use heightmaps is also covered.

Chapter 5, Controlling the Weather, includes essential configurations to control the different weather elements that can be used to create different weather moods.

Chapter 6, Working with Lumion Materials, helps you fully understand how to control materials and use special materials for special situations. Also, it covers how you can use materials to enhance the 3D world and correct some common errors.

Chapter 7, Special Features, gives you the knowledge to create special effects and learn how they contribute to enhance the final output.

Chapter 8, Getting Realism with Camera Effects, provides you with practical information to make the best use of several camera effects in order to achieve an amazing and realistic look for your still images and movies.

Chapter 9, Non-photorealistic Effects, explores some ways to create architectural visualizations with a non-photorealistic look and conceptual and technical illustrations.

Chapter 10, Bringing Your World to Life, explores how to turn a lifeless 3D world into a vibrant world full of animations and life. Some technical and advanced tools are also covered to give you full control over Lumion's camera.

Chapter 11, Creating Videos, gives you additional information about animation, but in particular, it provides information on how to create, organize, and combine small animation clips to create a beautiful movie.

Chapter 12, Rendering, shows you several crucial techniques to export and render movies, individual clips, single images, and image sequences.

Chapter 13, Lighting, helps you understand how you can use Lumion's lights to create perfect interior renders.

What you need for this book

Lumion Version 4 is used for all examples in this book; thus, you should have this version of Lumion to be able to follow the recipes contained in this book.

Who this book is for

This book is written with casual and professional artists in mind. With that said, it is important that you have some basic knowledge of Lumion and some digital content creation tools such as Photoshop and SketchUp.

Sections

This book contains the following sections:

Getting ready

This section tells us what to expect in the recipe, and describes how to set up any software or any preliminary settings needed for the recipe.

How to do it...

This section characterizes the steps to be followed for "cooking" the recipe.

How it works...

This section usually consists of a brief and detailed explanation of what happened in the previous section.

There's more...

It consists of additional information about the recipe in order to make the reader more anxious about the recipe.

See also

This section may contain references to the recipe.

Conventions

In this book, you will find a number of styles of text that distinguish between different kinds of information. Here are some examples of these styles, and an explanation of their meaning.

Code words in text, database table names, folder names, filenames, file extensions, pathnames, dummy URLs, user input, and Twitter handles are shown as follows: "Launch `Lumion.exe` located in the `Lumion` folder, or use the shortcut on the desktop."

New terms and **important words** are shown in bold. Words that you see on the screen, in menus or dialog boxes for example, appear in the text like this: "Select the **Edit materials** menu."

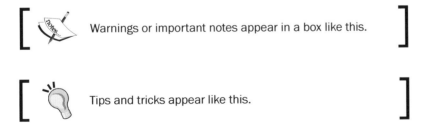

> Warnings or important notes appear in a box like this.

> Tips and tricks appear like this.

Reader feedback

Feedback from our readers is always welcome. Let us know what you think about this book—what you liked or may have disliked. Reader feedback is important for us to develop titles that you really get the most out of.

To send us general feedback, simply send an e-mail to feedback@packtpub.com and mention the book title via the subject of your message.

If there is a topic that you have expertise in and you are interested in either writing or contributing to a book, see our author guide on www.packtpub.com/authors.

Customer support

Now that you are the proud owner of a Packt book, we have a number of things to help you get the most from your purchase.

Downloading the color images of this book

We also provide you a PDF file that has color images of the screenshots/diagrams used in this book. The color images will help you better understand the changes in the output. You can download this file from https://www.packtpub.com/sites/default/files/downloads/0937OT_GraphicsBundle.pdf.

The resultant graphics from the recipes can also be seen at www.cirocardoso.net/lumion/.

Errata

Although we have taken every care to ensure the accuracy of our content, mistakes do happen. If you find a mistake in one of our books—maybe a mistake in the text or the code—we would be grateful if you would report this to us. By doing so, you can save other readers from frustration and help us improve subsequent versions of this book. If you find any errata, please report them by visiting http://www.packtpub.com/submit-errata, selecting your book, clicking on the **errata submission form** link, and entering the details of your errata. Once your errata are verified, your submission will be accepted and the errata will be uploaded on our website, or added to any list of existing errata, under the Errata section of that title. Any existing errata can be viewed by selecting your title from http://www.packtpub.com/support.

Piracy

Piracy of copyright material on the Internet is an ongoing problem across all media. At Packt, we take the protection of our copyright and licenses very seriously. If you come across any illegal copies of our works, in any form, on the Internet, please provide us with the location address or website name immediately so that we can pursue a remedy.

Please contact us at `copyright@packtpub.com` with a link to the suspected pirated material.

We appreciate your help in protecting our authors, and our ability to bring you valuable content.

Questions

You can contact us at `questions@packtpub.com` if you are having a problem with any aspect of the book, and we will do our best to address it.

1
Importing in Lumion

In this chapter, we will cover the following recipes:

- ▸ Importing your own 3D models
- ▸ Importing animations from 3ds Max
- ▸ Navigating in Lumion
- ▸ Relocating your imported 3D models
- ▸ Reverting your last action
- ▸ Locking your 3D model's position
- ▸ Organizing your 3D world with layers
- ▸ Updating your imported 3D models
- ▸ Replacing an imported 3D model

Introduction

Welcome to the first chapter of *Lumion 3D Cookbook*, which will assist you in developing and improving your workflow in Lumion. The main focus of this opening chapter will be in getting your 3D model properly imported in Lumion and your 3D scene organized. The nine recipes mentioned in the beginning of this chapter will cover some basic concepts that will help you to get an excellent and strong foundation for building the entire 3D world on top of it. As you will find throughout this Cookbook, Lumion is a powerful application, but the most significant aspect that you need to keep in mind is not to be afraid to experiment and have fun. Be curious and when reading one of these recipes, ask yourself what if, and this will help you to master Lumion.

Importing your own 3D models

Lumion supports a direct import of SketchUp files, which means that we don't need to use any special format to have our 3D model in Lumion. But if you are working with modeling packages, such as 3ds Max, Maya, and Blender, you need to use a different approach by exporting a COLLADA or FBX file as these two are the best formats to work with Lumion.

Getting ready

COLLADA is an XML namespace and database schema that allows you to move 3D files between 3ds Max, Maya, Revit, and Lumion. Each application is different, but in most cases, we just need to export or save our scene as a COLLADA file or an FBX file.

How to do it...

Let's start by launching Lumion with the following steps:

1. Launch `Lumion.exe` located in the `Lumion` folder, or use the shortcut on the desktop. You will be presented with an interface, as shown in the following screenshot:

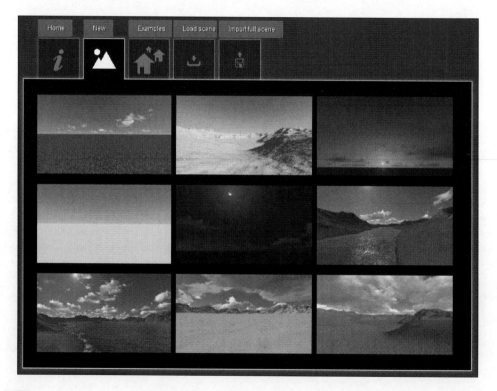

2. From the **New** tab, select one of the nine different presets to begin your new project, or just use the **Grass** scene to start with a basic scene. Each scene only differs in the type of weather, time of day, and terrain; nothing you couldn't get with a few minutes of work.

3. From the left-hand side of the screen, select the **Import** menu and click on the **Add a new model** button, as you can see in the following screenshot:

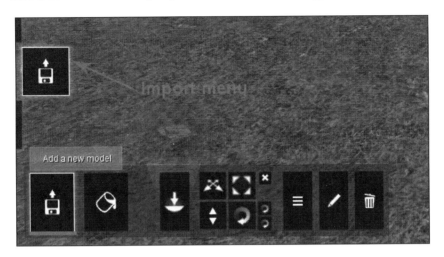

4. In the new window, navigate to where your 3D model it is, select it, and click the **Open** button. You may need to select the proper object file extension if you are not seeing the file.

5. Give a specific name for your imported model, or you can just leave the default name and click on the **Add to library** button.

6. Use your mouse and the keyboard shortcuts to navigate around your scene, and left-click to place the 3D model inside Lumion.

There's more...

This recipe is a really straightforward task as you can see, but is one of the most important tasks once you start working with Lumion. It is at this stage that you can be sure that everything is OK with your 3D model and make sure that you don't have any missing faces or other geometry problems. This step also assists you in checking if you have worked with the correct scale, so if your model is either extremely large or very small, you need to go back to your 3D modeling package and correct the scale. With all these things in mind, we now have a good base to start working with Lumion.

Another tip; we sometimes overlook the reality that even though Lumion is a very powerful application and can handle millions of polygons, it still has limits. So, if initially you just want to organize and populate your scene without paying too much consideration to the 3D model itself, it is good to create a proxy or a simple representation of your 3D model and import that proxy, and then later with a special feature in Lumion, reimport your high-poly model.

See also

▶ To import animations, check the *Importing animations from 3ds Max* recipe in this chapter

▶ To help you navigate in Lumion, have a look at the *Navigating in Lumion* recipe in this chapter

Importing animations from 3ds Max

In particular situations, we may need to use our own animations. You may be aware that we can import basic animations in Lumion from 3D modeling packages such as 3ds Max. This recipe is going to help us to understand how we can import such animations and the limitations associated with these external animations.

Getting ready

Prior to importing an animation into Lumion, we need to check a few things first. Lumion doesn't support vertex, morph, and bone animations, and we can only bring in basic animations on the move, rotate, and scale values. The **frames per second** (**FPS**) rate needs to be set to 25, and you can export your animation as an FBX file or DAE file, although with the last option, the interpolation between key frames will be linear, so bear that in mind.

How to do it...

With Lumion launched, perform the following steps:

1. On the left-hand side of the screen, select the **Import** menu and click on the **Add a new model** button.

2. In the new window, navigate to where you have your 3D model, select it, and click on the **Open** button.

3. Give a specific name to your imported model, or you can just leave the default name, and select the **Import animations** checkbox, as you can see in the following screenshot:

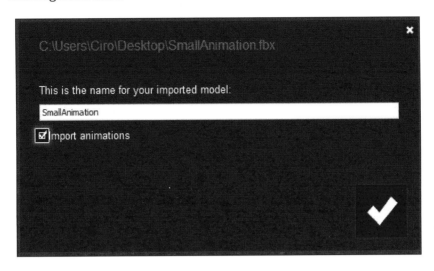

4. Click on the **Add to library** button to import your 3D model.

5. Use your mouse and the keyboard shortcuts to navigate around your scene, and left-click to place the 3D model inside Lumion.

6. After placing the 3D model, you can see the animation going in a loop, which means that you will need to use some **Layers** effects in order to control these external animations.

There's more...

It's true that Lumion allows you to import simple animations, but most of the time, this is not the best solution. Why? First, once the animation is in Lumion, you have little control over it, and second, only basic animations with the move, rotate, and scale values are possible in Lumion. It's true that we can use a specific layer to switch the animation on and off when required or use the **Objects** effect to control the position of the animation, but we still have limited control.

However, there is one particular situation when we may import an animation from Maya or 3ds Max. It's when we have a walk cycle of a person that we want to use in Lumion, and in this circumstance, we import this object along with the walk cycle and use the **Advance move** effect or the **Move** effect to control it.

In animation, a walk cycle is a series of frames or illustrations drawn in a sequence that loops to create an animation of a walking character. The walk cycle is looped over and over, thus having to avoid animating each step again.

Navigating in Lumion

Lumion uses the flexibility of shortcuts to improve the control we have in the 3D world. This recipe will focus on how to use some of these shortcuts to improve the workflow and the way we control Lumion's camera.

How to do it...

With Lumion launched and with a scene open, perform the following steps:

1. To look around, right-click and move the mouse to look inside your 3D world, and if you want to reset the camera to the horizontal viewpoint, use the combination *Ctrl + H*. In the **Settings** menu, you can invert this action by activating the **Enable Inverted Up\Down Camera Pan** option.

2. The arrow keys along with the combination *WSAD* are used to move the camera, and the keys *Q* and *E* are used to move the camera up and down.

3. Use the middle mouse button to pan the camera; this gives you very accurate control.

4. Press the Space bar key along with the arrow keys or with the combination *WSAD* to slowly move the camera.

5. Lumion has a sort of zoom on to the object option that we can use by double-clicking with the right mouse button on a model or even on the ground.

There's more...

The reason why we bring up these shortcuts is that when working with the **Photo** and **Video** modes, we need a more precise and accurate way to move the camera to create the perfect composition. However, there is an additional option that will be very handy in the final stages when we want to produce a movie or a still image.

That's the option to save and load the specific camera viewpoints. Use the *Ctrl + 0, 1, 2, 3, 4, 5, 6, 7, 8,* or *9* to save up to 10 camera positions and the combination *Shift + 0, 1, 2, 3, 4, 5, 6, 7, 8,* or *9* to load the saved camera viewpoints. Then we can use these saved viewpoints in the **Photo** mode, as shown in the following screenshot where each thumbnail represents the camera viewpoint saved previously:

Relocating your imported 3D models

Once we import a 3D model or even if we use a model from the Lumion library, we need to adjust the position, the orientation, and the scale of the 3D model. But keep in mind the importance of organizing your 3D world using layers as well. They are free and they will become very useful when we need to hide some objects to focus our attention on a specific detail or when we use the **Hide layer** and **Show layer** effect.

Getting ready

If we want to rearrange a 3D model that is imported, choose the **Import** menu, but if we need to move a model in the Lumion library, select the **Objects** menu. In both situations, we are going to use the same steps, so I will just use the expression "3D model" to refer to both the models.

How to do it...

With our scene opened, perform the following steps:

1. Select the 3D model, and if you need to select multiple objects, use the combination *Ctrl*+ the left mouse button to draw a rectangular selection.
2. Press the *M* key to move the 3D model.
3. To place the 3D model on the ground, press the *G* key.
4. If you are moving the 3D model in a terrain with variations, press the *Shift* key to turn off the horizontal snapping.
5. If you want to copy the selected objects and paste them in a different location, press the *Alt* key while moving your objects.

6. Don't forget that we can use the *L* key to scale the 3D model, the *R* key to rotate the object, and the *H* key to move the 3D model vertically, as you can see in the following screenshot:

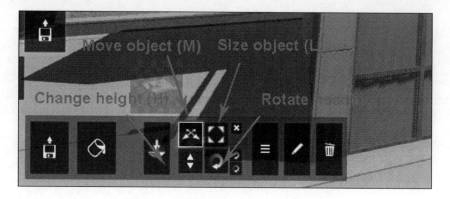

Another option that is more accurate is as follows:

1. In the **Import** or **Objects** menu, select the **Edit properties** submenu.

2. Select the 3D model.

3. In the 3D model properties window, type in the new coordinates, as you can see in the following screenshot:

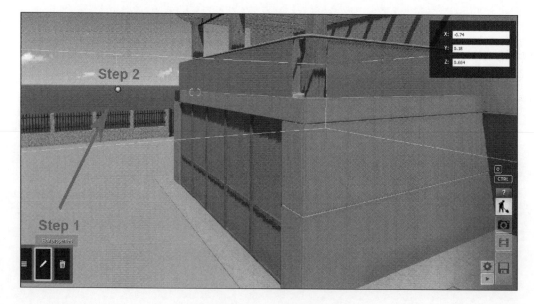

How it works...

If our 3D model is not moving and we didn't lock it, this is because we have the wrong category selected. This means, for example, that in order to move a tree we need to select the **Nature** category.

There's more...

Here is a tip to help us improve the workflow while placing and moving the 3D models. We may know where we want the trees or other 3D models to be placed, and sometimes we have the freedom to choose this, but in most cases, we will get a landscape project with this information. While working in the 3D package (3ds Max, Maya, or SketchUp), create small cubes (100 mm x 100 mm) with different colors that correspond to different elements. They can represent a specific type of tree, bushes, hedges, flowers, and lamps, and we import these small cubes with the 3D model in Lumion.

In Lumion, create a top view with the camera (don't forget to save it using the combination *Ctrl + 0, 1* to 9) and with the aid of this viewpoint, we can start composing a 3D world and place the trees and other objects where the small cubes are. Then, if necessary, assign the invisible material to these cubes to hide them. With this workflow, we can be sure that everything is in the correct place and we don't need to lose time arranging the entire scene. Oh and don't forget to use layers; we will cover some recipes later that will help you with this.

See also

> ▶ To organize your 3D world with layers, check the *Organizing your 3D world with layers* recipe in this chapter

Reverting your last action

At a certain point in our project, we will need to go back and undo a mistake or something that doesn't look as expected. Lumion offers you a very limited undo option. Let's see how it works.

Getting ready

This option depends on which menu you have selected, because in some menus, such as the **Weather** menu, you can't find it at all.

How to do it...

With our scene opened, perform the following steps:

1. Right-click on the model to place a model or to change the terrain.

2. To revert this last action, click on the **Undo** button that you will find at the bottom of the menu, as shown in the following screenshot:

3. As you can see, in the previous recipe, we used the **Move object** tool to move the 3D model and the **Undo** button appears, giving us the opportunity to undo the movement.

There's more...

That's it? Yes, and as you can see, this undo feature is very limited. I trust that in the future versions of Lumion, we will get a little more than just one single undo. However, the rationale for introducing this easy recipe is to show you the two ways to overcome this restriction.

The first option is using the *F5* key to do a quick save before importing a model or changing an object's position, but unfortunately, there is no option to do a quick load. The second option saves various versions of your work, particularly when doing a big change, such as replacing all the trees for another type, changing the environment or the landscape. By saving various versions, we can always go back to a specific point and start over.

So, this undo option is very limited, and the only time I really wish to have more flexibility is when I am modeling a terrain, but have a look at the following recipe to help you with modeling a terrain.

See also

▶ To have more control over the terrain, have a look at the *Working with heightmaps* recipe in *Chapter 4, Constructing Your World*

Locking your 3D model's position

When working with Lumion, and in particular, when organizing our 3D world, and arranging and adjusting the 3D models, we might find the possibility of locking the 3D model's position to be useful. This helps us to avoid selecting and unintentionally moving other, already placed 3D models.

Getting ready

To get prepared, you need to select your 3D model or multiple models, and for that don't forget to use the **Context** menu that we can find inside the **Import** and **Objects** menu.

How to do it...

With the 3D model or models selected, perform the following steps:

1. Select the **Context** menu.
2. Chose the **Transformation** submenu.
3. Select the **Lock position...** option.
4. Click on the **On** option to lock, or the **Off** option to unlock, as you can see in the following screenshot:

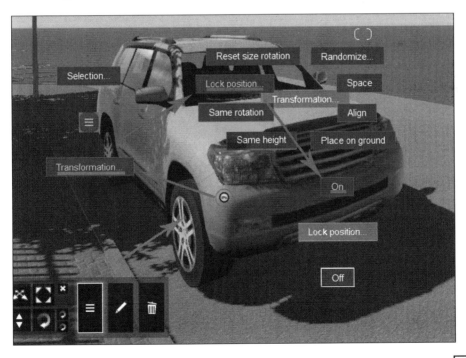

There's more...

Another way to guarantee that our 3D models are locked and we don't move them accidentally is using layers and then hiding them while we work with 3D models.

Organizing your 3D world with layers

From the beginning of our project with Lumion, it is very important for us to organize and categorize our 3D world. Sometimes we may not do this straightaway, and only after importing some 3D models and adding some content from the Lumion library we realize the need to organize our project in a better way. So, we are going to see how to use layers and how to assign the existing 3D models to a new layer.

Getting ready

Remember that the **Layer** menu will only appear when we have the **Import** or **Objects** menu selected.

How to do it...

With our scene opened, perform the following steps:

1. Select the **Import** or **Objects** menu.
2. On the top-left corner of the screen, you can locate the **Layer** menu, as shown in the following screenshot:

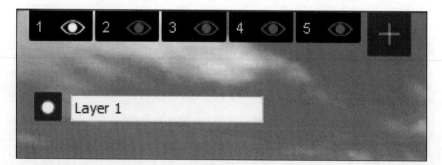

3. Select the **Layer 1** option and rename it for something more precise, such as `Trees`.
4. With this layer selected, go to the **Objects** menu.
5. Add a tree to your scene.
6. At this moment, the tree you added is inside the layer `Trees`, and you can hide or show this layer by clicking on the icon that represents an eye.

If you want to add a 3D model to a layer, perform the following steps:

1. Select the 3D model.

2. Go to the **Layer** menu and select the correct layer.

3. Use the **Move selection to layer** button to move your 3D model to the layer you want, as you can see in the following screenshot:

We can create up to 20 layers, which gives plenty of room to make full use of the layers feature. Don't forget that in order to use these layers, we need to select the correct layer before placing or importing a 3D model of our scene; otherwise, the 3D models will be placed in the first layer or the layer you have selected. Having our scene arranged with layers will also help us to know if our workstation is starting to struggle with the amount of 3D models we have in Lumion, and switching off a few layers will give us a little room to breathe and improve the speed.

See also

▶ To control the layers, check the *Animating the layers* recipe in *Chapter 10, Bringing Your World to Life*

Updating your imported 3D models

Over the course of a project, it is very common to have certain 3D models updated, and we need to update those 3D models into our Lumion project. This can be a rather daunting task, taking into account that most of the time these updates in the 3D models happen after we have already assigned materials to the imported 3D model.

Getting ready

Before we update the 3D model into Lumion, it is vital that we save or export the 3D model with the same name that we used to import into Lumion. This means that we need to overwrite the old file (we can always create a backup) so that we can update the 3D model in Lumion successfully.

How to do it...

With the **Import** menu selected, perform the following steps:

1. Select the **Edit materials** menu.

2. Then click on the small white dot on the 3D model to select the model.

3. Click on the **Reload model and re apply materials** button, as you can see in the following screenshot:

4. Click on the **OK** button to accept the changes.

There's more...

As a safety practice, we might want to save our old files in case something goes wrong. Typically, I rename the file to something like `House_OLD_01-13.dae` (`.dae` is the extension for the COLLADA files and is just for reference purposes). The `OLD` tag is self-explanatory, showing that this is an old file and the `01-13` tag represents the month and the year it was created. If the project is complex and there are a few modifications, just create a text file where the 3D models are stored, and in this text file write something like the following:

- ▸ `House_OLD_01-13.dae -> Fence replaced`
- ▸ `House_OLD_02-13.dae-> Window ground floor replaced`

Why should we go this extra mile and do this? Well, the reason is that when we are working on large projects, they can take weeks and even months to be completed, and a complex project always goes forward and back with changes, which means that something you changed last month may be back after a few weeks because the client changed their mind. With this text file we don't need to open every single file to check where we did the change.

Replacing an imported 3D model

Sometimes during the project we may face a radical change in a 3D model we have already imported into the Lumion project. The worst scenario is reassigning all the materials to the new 3D model and perhaps relocating to the correct place. However, Lumion has an option to help us with this and to avoid reassigning all the materials or at least not all of them, and the 3D model will stay in exactly the same place.

Getting ready

Before we begin replacing the 3D model, we may want to save another version just in case something goes wrong, and another safety measure is saving a material set as a backup.

How to do it...

With the **Import** menu selected, perform the following steps:

1. Select the **Edit materials** menu.
2. Click on the small white dot on our 3D model to select the model.
3. On the bottom-right corner of the screen, we can see the **Reload model and re apply materials** button.

4. Press the *Ctrl* key to activate the **Reload model and re apply materials new file** button, as you can see in the following screenshot:

5. Click on the **Reload model and re apply materials new file** button to open a new window.

6. Select the file and click on the **Open** button.

7. Click on the **OK** button to accept the changes.

There's more...

In most situations, this will work as long we don't modify the names of the objects inside the 3D file. What that means is, for example, we can change the size, rotation, and even the position of the wall_01 object, and when we reload the model, the material that was assigned to the wall_01 object will be the same. However, if you change the name of the object for something like Wall_01, just the fact that you used a capital letter will be enough to confuse Lumion, and the material will not be assigned.

See also

▶ To save the materials assigned to the model, check the *Saving materials* recipe found in *Chapter 6, Working With Lumion Materials*

2
Placing the Content

In this chapter, we will cover the following recipes:

- ▶ Placing 3D models
- ▶ Copying 3D models
- ▶ Removing 3D models
- ▶ Placing models on the terrain
- ▶ Placing multiple 3D models
- ▶ Randomizing the size of the 3D models
- ▶ Configuring 3D models
- ▶ Placing 3D models accurately

Introduction

After learning how to import and rearrange 3D models in Lumion, it is time to turn our attention to the extraordinary collection of 3D models that comes along with Lumion. Lumion Pro gives us access to more than 2,000 3D models, such as trees, cars, houses, people, animals, interior furniture, and other 3D models ready to go, which, in most cases, cover the common needs of a project. However, if necessary, we can import our own models.

The title of this chapter is called *Placing the Content* because we will explore and work with the majority of the tools we need, not only to place 3D models from the Lumion library, but also to provide some tips to help populate the 3D world with content so diverse that it will enhance our final image or video.

Placing 3D models

After importing a 3D model we created in our favorite 3D modeling package, it is likely that we want to enhance the look and the environment of the project by using additional 3D models. The lack of detail and content will definitely create a lifeless and dull image or video. This recipe will not only help you learn how to place content from the Lumion library, but also how you can discover what you need.

Getting ready

Before you begin, you need to have Lumion open. Though this can be a little repetitive, create a specific layer for each category that you are going to use.

How to do it...

To start placing content, perform the following steps:

1. On the left-hand side of the screen, select the **Objects** menu. At the bottom of the menu, you can see the different categories of 3D models that you can add to your 3D world. If you hover your mouse over each button, a small pop up appears, which tells you the type of models you can find inside that library.

2. As an example, select the **Nature** category.

3. By default, there is an object already selected, and to change this 3D model, you need to click on the thumbnail with the 3D model called **Change object**, as you can see in the following screenshot:

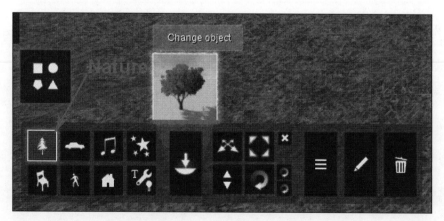

4. The **Nature Library** window is seen with all the accessible content in the **Nature** category.

5. You may feel a little overwhelmed by the number of 3D models available, but everything is arranged in 12 tabs, and each tab can have one or more pages with 3D models.

6. You can move the mouse over the thumbnail to get more information about the 3D model.

7. With the left mouse button, choose a 3D model—this selection will take you back to the **Build** menu.

8. Click again with the left mouse button to place one copy of the 3D model.

9. You can go back to the **Nature Library** window and select a different 3D model or change the category.

There's more...

We used a tree as an example, but the Lumion library has a lot more to offer you. So, take some time to explore the different tabs and categories and see for yourself what is offered. Having an idea of what is available in the Lumion library is quite useful because while we are modeling the building, we can think in advance of how to save some time by using the content found in the Lumion library. One thing you can do is create a .pdf file with all the 3D models you can find in Lumion and use this document while planning and modeling your environment. It is tedious to take a screenshot of every tab and every category, but it is quite useful while planning and thinking of the 3D elements needed for the project.

Other elements you can find among the different 3D models are basic animations. We can find some useful animations, such as flying birds, butterflies, falling leaves, swimming fish, and walking and talking people. We will focus our attention on the people section, though initially we may find it strange that even if we add a walking man or a woman to our project, they keep walking in the same place. This makes perfect sense because it allows more control on what you are doing. Thus, when we create a video later, we have the opportunity to control the path and the direction using the **Advance mode** effect under the **Movie** mode.

See also

▸ To see how to import a 3D model, refer to the *Importing your own 3D models* and *Importing animations from 3ds Max* recipes in *Chapter 1, Importing in Lumion*

▸ To work with the 3D models' animations, refer to the *Bringing people to life* recipe in *Chapter 10, Bringing Your World to Life*

Copying 3D models

Something indispensable for a smooth workflow in every project are the copy and paste tools. Imagine having to go to the import library to place the 3D model again and assigning a material every single time we need a 3D model. Lumion doesn't have a standard copy and paste tool that we can find in most software, but there is a way to emulate this feature. This recipe will help you copy a 3D model already present in your scene and avoid the trouble of going back to the Lumion library and placing a 3D model already present in your project.

Getting ready

You should have already opened Lumion. Locate the 3D model you want to copy.

How to do it...

To start copying the content, perform the following steps:

1. Select the **Objects** menu.

2. Press the *M* key to select the move tool.

3. Make sure that you have the correct category selected; otherwise, you may not be able to select the model you want.

4. Press the *Alt* key, and with the left mouse button, select the 3D model and drag to make a copy, as shown in the following screenshot:

5. You can also click-and-drag the 3D model first and then press the *Alt* key to make a copy.

6. After this, you can use the move, rotate, and scale tools to adjust the 3D model that has been copied.

There's more...

The same principle applies to duplicate a 3D model we have imported. A practical scenario where we can use this feature is when we have an area with several houses and they look precisely look the same. To save some time, we may feel tempted to import all the 3D models in one single file. Although there is nothing wrong with that, even with a good workstation, Lumion may struggle with so much information that it could crash or stop responding. Instead, we can export one 3D model and duplicate it in Lumion using the feature mentioned in this recipe.

See also

▶ If you need to replace or update an imported 3D model, see the *Updating your imported 3D models* and *Replacing an imported 3D model* recipes in *Chapter 1, Importing in Lumion*

Removing 3D models

Removing or deleting a 3D model is a part of the process of any project. This can be particularly tricky when our 3D world is crowded with 3D models and there is a possibility of selecting and deleting the wrong 3D model. Nevertheless, Lumion does a great job in this area because it protects you from deleting something by mistake.

Getting ready

Locate the 3D model you want to delete, and according to your situation, you may need to select either the **Import** or the **Objects** menu.

How to do it...

To remove a 3D model from your project, perform the following steps:

1. Select the correct category first from the **Objects** menu, or use the **Import** menu to work with an imported 3D model.

2. From the menu that you find at the bottom of your screen, select the **Trash object** button that looks like a trash bin, as shown in the following screenshot:

3. With this option selected, click on the small white dot with the left mouse button to delete the object.

4. To delete multiple objects, you need to select them first and then click on the small white dot to delete all the selected 3D models.

5. The quickest way to select multiple objects is selecting one of the tools, such as the **Move** tool, then pressing the *Ctrl* key and dragging it with the left mouse button to draw a rectangle around the 3D models.

There's more...

If you have deleted a 3D model by mistake, you can always use the **Undo** button that appears next to the **Trash object** button, but keep in mind that you can only go back once. In order to avoid unnecessary problems and difficulties while deleting 3D models from our project, it is always good practice to lock the 3D models that don't need any modification at the moment or are already placed in the correct position. This action will not only help you to avoid deleting them by mistake, but also to avoid changing their position, and this can happen particularly when we have a packed scene and it's tricky to understand what we are selecting and deleting.

▸ To lock the 3D models in your project, have a look at the *Locking your 3D model's position* recipe in *Chapter 1, Importing in Lumion*

Placing models on the terrain

All projects are different, and this typically brings in unique challenges. Sometimes, a building or the environment are really intricate, and this can cause difficulties when we are placing 3D models from the Lumion library. Lumion recognizes surfaces and will avoid intersecting them with any 3D model you want to place in your world. However, there are times when this feature may be in our way and cause difficulties when placing a 3D model. Let's see how we can solve that.

Getting ready

To follow the example in this recipe, you should have a 3D model placed in your project; for example, to follow this recipe, you can use a table or bench to see how to place a 3D model.

How to do it...

To start placing content, perform the following steps:

1. On the left-hand side of the screen, select the **Objects** menu. Here, you will find different categories of 3D models to add to your 3D world.

2. As an example, select the **Outdoor** category. This will open the **Outdoor Library** window with all the content available in this class.

3. In the example used in this recipe, I selected the **GardenTable_003** option from the **Assorted** tab.

4. After placing the garden table, we can add some books, and you can find some of them under the **Furniture** tab.

5. Before placing the 3D model, you can see a yellow box that represents the 3D model along with a red dimension line that informs you of the height where you are placing the 3D model.

6. To force Lumion to place the book on the terrain, press and hold the G key and note that even if you put the mouse over a surface, Lumion will ignore it and put the 3D model on the terrain. This is shown in the following screenshot:

7. Press and hold the G key to force the placing of the 3D model on the ground, and click with the left mouse button to place one copy of the 3D model.

There's more...

There are some specific situations when this feature will become very handy. As mentioned in the beginning of this recipe, some projects are very complex—we need to fill plants, flowers, or rocks in a precise manner. Due the nature of the building, we may find it difficult and frustrating to place the 3D models close to edges because Lumion starts to get confused where we want to place the 3D model because it avoids intersecting of surfaces.

Placing multiple 3D models

A project needs life, but placing dozens of models one by one is a massive task. Lumion helps us to populate our 3D world by providing the option to place more than one copy at a time. By means of a shortcut, we can place 10 copies of a 3D model.

Getting ready

Before you begin, you need to have Lumion open and the right layer selected to place the 3D model.

How to do it...

To place 10 copies of a 3D model, perform the following steps:

1. Select the 3D model you want to place either from the Lumion library or a 3D model you already imported.

2. Hold the *Ctrl* key and click with the left mouse button to place 10 scattered copies of the 3D model, as you can see in the following screenshot:

3. Click again on any other point of your 3D project if you want to add 10 more copies.

There's more...

This is a feature that I use with a few 3D models and in specific situations. Why? As you can see in the preceding screenshot, it is true that we can place 10 copies of a 3D model at once. However, that is all you can do. Consequently, you have very narrow control. We don't have control over the area that the 3D models are scattered and also the distance between them. Again, in our example, two bushes are intersecting, and although in this case it is not a big issue, most of the time you wouldn't want this to happen. So, in reality, we have two options, that is, we use this feature and then manually move the 3D models that are intersecting, or we place the 3D models one by one.

Randomizing the size of 3D models

The world we live in is bursting with diversity and variety. Consequently, our eyes are incredible in picking up repetitions. Sometimes, even if we cannot explain why, we know something is wrong with a picture because it doesn't look natural. When we are working on a big project, such repetitions stand out almost immediately. We can use a feature in Lumion that gives us the ability to randomize the size of 3D models while placing them.

Getting ready

Remember that we cannot randomize the size of 3D models already present in the scene. This will only work while placing 3D models from the Lumion library.

How to do it...

To randomize the scale of a 3D model while placing it, perform the following steps:

1. From the **Import** or **Objects** menu, select your 3D model.
2. Press the Z key.
3. Start by placing the 3D model using the left mouse button.
4. This works best when you are placing multiple 3D models, as you can see in the following screenshot:

5. With some 3D models, you may not spot the difference immediately, such as plants and 3D models from the **Nature** category, but in the examples used in the preceding screenshot, it is easy to see how this process works.
6. Also, with some 3D models, it will not only randomize the size, but also the color, as you can see in the preceding screenshot.

There's more...

This is a really useful feature that will help us enhance our scene with plenty of variety. Here is a small trick that allows you to place 10 copies of a specific 3D model and, at the same time, randomize their size. Press the *Z* and *Ctrl* keys at the same time and use the left mouse button to place the 3D model.

Configuring 3D models

With more than 2,000 models, we can say that Lumion has everything we need to use in our project. Although Lumion has predefined models, it doesn't mean that we can't modify some basic options. Let's see how we can modify simple settings such as color and texture, but keep in mind that this doesn't mean we can change these settings in every single 3D model.

Getting ready

Before you begin, you need to have some 3D models placed in your project.

How to do it...

For this recipe, let's use a tree as an example:

1. Select the **Objects** menu on the left-hand side of the screen.
2. Click on the **Edit properties** menu and select the tree.
3. The **Tree Properties** window will appear, as shown in the following screenshot:

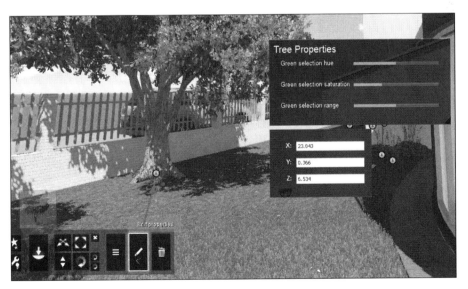

4. Adjust the **Green selection hue** setting to change the color of the leaves and use values above **1**; otherwise, you will end up with purple trees.

5. Adjust the **Green selection saturation** setting to control the overall saturation.

6. Adjust the **Green selection range** setting.

We can also change the color of a car with the following steps:

1. Select the **Objects** menu on the left-hand side of the screen.

2. Click on the **Edit properties** menu and select the car.

3. The **Vehicle Color** window appears where you can change the color, as shown in the following screenshot:

There's more...

It is difficult to tell you which 3D models can be modified. We could say that almost 90 percent of the 3D models in Lumion can be changed, and we will find a wide range of settings. We have simple activities such as changing the color of a car and changing the texture of a flag, and more complex activities such as configuring a fire, smoke, or fog. A good suggestion is to take some time and explore the Lumion library, and this will help you even before starting modeling.

Placing 3D models accurately

In almost every project, we have some autonomy to place the 3D models and organize the 3D world. Nevertheless, there are times when we really need more accuracy than one can get with the mouse. Let's see how Lumion's coordinate system can assist us with this task.

Getting ready

Locate the 3D model you want to place in your project and make sure it is not locked.

How to do it...

To place a 3D model accurately, perform the following steps:

1. From the **Import** or **Objects** menu, select the 3D model.

2. After placing the 3D model, click on the **Edit properties** menu.

3. Select the 3D model and a window appears where you can see the **X:, Y:,** and **Z:** coordinates, as shown in the following screenshot:

4. Adjust the coordinates to accurately move the 3D model to the correct place.

How it works...

Lumion uses the XYZ coordinate system to place the 3D models, and the center of your world is at 0, 0, 0 respectively. That is why when you import a 3D model, occasionally you can't see it because when you model the house, you did it far away from the 0, 0, 0 point.

There's more...

This distinctive feature is handy in reality when we have a heavy 3D scene. Let's pick up an example of a housing estate; however, we now have 10 different houses, and we are having difficulties importing them in Lumion. A workaround for this is instead of exporting the entire scene, we can export the 10 houses individually and assemble them in Lumion. But how do you know where to put everything back? The coordinate system can be really useful in a situation like this.

First, make a habit of modeling the building or whatever you want at the 0, 0, 0 coordinates in your 3D modeling package. Second, create a group for every single 3D model you want to export, and after that, check the coordinates for those groups on the 3D modeling package. Third, move all the groups to the center point, or in other words, to the 0, 0, 0 coordinates and export them. Fourth, while importing the 3D models into Lumion, you already know where these are supposed to be and, using the coordinate system, you can move each house to the correct place.

3

Manipulating and Controlling 3D Models

In this chapter, we will cover the following recipes:

- ▶ Selecting multiple 3D models
- ▶ Selecting different categories
- ▶ Transforming and selecting any 3D model
- ▶ Spacing multiple 3D models
- ▶ Aligning different 3D models' orientations
- ▶ Snapping multiple 3D models
- ▶ Randomizing 3D models' orientation
- ▶ Rotate on model
- ▶ Constraining the 3D model's rotation

Introduction

Now that we've mastered the Lumion basics, we can move on to another indispensable stage in any project. It is challenging to describe where this stage starts and ends, but controlling the 3D models and modifying their appearance is crucial if we want to add life to a project. We will be doing this even in the final steps before exporting a still image or a video.

A good deal of the tools covered in this chapter are simple to use, but are important to perform tasks to change the look and size of a 3D model—just to mention the most basic ones. Although we will cover how to control and manipulate Lumion's native 3D models in great detail, the same principle and tools are used to control the 3D models we imported.

Selecting multiple 3D models

Typically, we focus our attention on selecting separate 3D models so that we can make exact and accurate adjustments. Eventually, we will need to do some alterations and modifications to multiple 3D objects. This recipe shows you how you can do this, along with a practical application of this recipe.

Getting ready

For this tutorial, you need to locate the 3D models you need to tweak; don't forget to select the correct category under the **Objects** menu. Also, keep in mind that to select and control a 3D model, you need to click on the small white dot under the 3D model.

How to do it...

To select multiple objects, perform the following steps:

1. On the left-hand side of the screen, select the **Objects** menu.

2. Select the right category for the 3D model you want to select. In this example, we want to select people, so we will select the **People and Animals** category.

3. If the **Place object** button is selected, you need to select another tool, such as the **Move object** tool or the **Context** menu for example.

4. Press and hold the *Ctrl* key, and with the left mouse button pressed, drag to draw a rectangle around the 3D model.

5. On the top-left corner of the rectangular selection, you can see the **Selection count** value that lets you know how many objects you have selected so far, as shown in the following screenshot:

Selection count : 3

6. Keep in mind that you need to pay some attention while selecting 3D models because while using this method, you may end up selecting other 3D models that are behind other 3D models or buildings.

7. Make the selection in the first attempt; if not, every time you press the left mouse button, you will deselect the previous selection.

8. You can make multiple selections while pressing the *Ctrl* key and by clicking on the small white dot under each 3D model.

9. Now that you have multiple 3D models selected, you can perform various tasks that you would normally do with just one 3D model, such as moving to a new position.

This is perhaps the simplest and quickest way to select multiple 3D models, but there is another way we can select multiple objects, as described in the following steps:

1. Select the **Context** menu and select a 3D model.

2. You have two options, but for this case, click on the **Selection...** submenu, and, as you can see in the following screenshot, several options will appear:

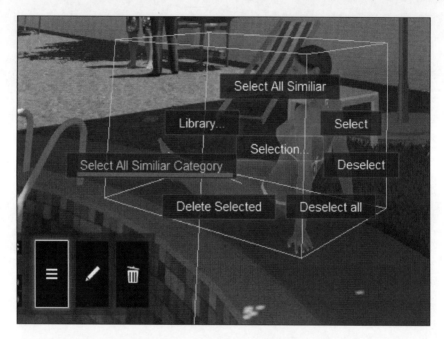

3. If you select the **Select All Similar Category** option, this will select all the 3D models that are in the same category.

4. If you select the **Select All Similar** option, this will only select those 3D models that are equal to the 3D model you selected.

There's more...

Keep in mind that there is a substantial difference between the options **Select All Similar** and **Select All Similar Category**. For example, if we use the **Select All Similar** option with a tree called **AfricanOlive2_RT**, Lumion selects all the **AfricanOlive2_RT** 3D models present in the project.

Now, if we use the **Select All Similar Category** option with the same **AfricanOlive2_RT** tree, Lumion selects all the 3D models inside the **Nature** category.

Selecting different categories

While working with selections in Lumion, every time we make a selection and transform the 3D model, we need to choose the correct category. There are particular occasions when we need to select and manipulate 3D models that belong to different categories. This recipe is going to show you a small trick to select 3D models from different categories in one go. Let's see how we can do that.

Getting ready

Before you start, make sure that the 3D models you want to move are not locked or hidden.

How to do it...

To select different categories, you just need to perform the following steps:

1. Open the **Objects** menu and pick a category to start selecting the 3D models.

2. Press and hold the *Ctrl* key and with the left mouse button and drag to draw a rectangle around the 3D models.

3. Select another category and hold the *Ctrl* key, but instead of dragging the mouse to draw a selection rectangle, you need to select each individual 3D model, as you can see in the following screenshot:

4. After selecting the 3D models, you can control them using the shortcuts *M* to move, *L* to scale, and *R* to rotate.

5. Select the **Context** menu to deselect all the selected items or use the **Deselect All** button, as shown in the following screenshot:

Transforming and selecting any 3D model

Initially, we may find Lumion very restrictive in the way it works with the content placed in our project because we need to select the correct category every time we want to work with a 3D model. However, we can bypass these restrictions by using the option to select and move any 3D model in our world without selecting a category. Let's see how we can do that.

Getting ready

To apply this recipe, check whether you don't have any 3D models locked, and keep in mind that if you are working with an imported model, you need to have the **Import** menu selected.

How to do it...

To select and transform any 3D model, perform the following steps:

1. Press the *F12* key, and you will see that the small dots that are used to select the 3D models disappear.

2. To select any 3D model, you just need to click on the 3D model with the left mouse button.

3. The following screenshot shows that even if you are in the **People and Animals** category, we can select a 3D model from the **Outdoor** category:

4. While selecting the 3D model, you can drag the mouse to move the 3D model, but you can perform other tasks.

5. Press and hold the *R* key and select another 3D model to change the orientation.

6. Press and hold the *H* key and select a 3D model to change the height.

7. Click on the **Context** menu to deactivate the *F12* option.

There's more...

When we press the key and activate the *F12* option to select any 3D model, Lumion not only identifies the 3D models present in the scene, but also the terrain and the sky, and this can be quite confusing, especially with a crowded scene. Although we can use the *F12* key to move, rotate, and change the height of a 3D model, we don't have the ability to change the size.

Spacing multiple 3D models

As mentioned earlier in this book, the world we live is full of diversity and randomness; however, almost on every project, there are some situations when we need to place the content in an orderly way. A quick example is when we need to place garden lamps along a path and they need to be spaced equally. Let's see how we can do that in Lumion.

Getting ready

Before you start, you need the 3D models already present in your project; make sure you have the quantity you need.

How to do it...

To space the selection of 3D models equally, perform the following steps:

1. Select the **Objects** menu on the left-hand side of the screen.
2. Select the 3D models by pressing and holding the *Ctrl* key and drag them with the left mouse button to do a multiple selection, or press the *Ctrl* key and with the left mouse button, manually select every single model you want.
3. Select the **Context** menu and click on the small white dot that is available for every 3D model.
4. Select the **Transformation...** submenu and select the **Space** option. This will evenly space them in a straight line, as you can see in the following screenshot:

5. After that, you can move the 3D models to a correct position or even adjust the rotation to fit in your project.

There's more...

This is a fantastic tool and a time saver, in particular when you are working on a commercial project where you have elements, such as lamp posts, parking bays, and other objects that need an equal distance between them.

The previous screenshot shows a practical example of how to apply this recipe, but there is a catch to achieve the same result. We can tell Lumion that we want to space out a certain number of 3D models along a specific distance. What we need to do is place a 3D model at the beginning of the parking bay and another on the other end and then place another three objects between them. Once you perform the steps mentioned in this recipe, you will have five lamp posts in the correct place; however, we need to select the first or the last model for this to work.

Aligning different 3D models' orientations

Lumion is a unique application not only because of what we can do with an incredible quality, but also because we have features that initially may not seem beneficial at all until we work on a project where we see a practical application. One example is when we need to align the orientations of different 3D models, and in this recipe, we will see not only how to use it, but also how to apply it in a practical situation.

Getting ready

Before we begin, you may want to use a top-view angle camera to better adjust the 3D models you want to use.

How to do it...

To align the orientation of two or more 3D models, perform the following steps:

1. Select the **Objects** menu and the correct category.
2. Press and hold the *Ctrl* key to perform multiple selections.
3. Select the **Context** menu and click on the **Transformation...** submenu.
4. Select the **Same Rotation** option to align the selected 3D models.

How it works...

We need to keep in mind that the model we select first has dictated the rotation used for all the 3D models selected. For example, have a look at the following screenshot:

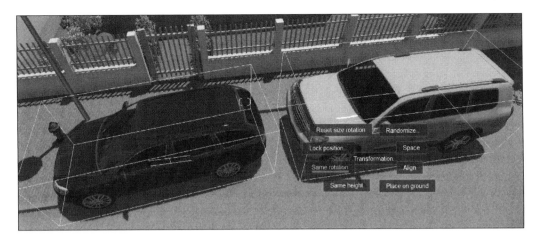

We want to align these two cars using the orientation from the white car. This means that when we select the 3D model, we need to select the white car first and then select the black car. Then, when we click on the **Same rotation** option, Lumion uses the white car's orientation to adjust the one for the black car.

There's more...

This is a simple and straightforward recipe, but is useful in some specific situations. Let's see one example of how we can apply this recipe for a commercial project. In this project, we need to have cars in the car park. However, when we look at the final result after placing all the cars, it surely looks computer generated because everything is perfectly aligned in the same orientation, as you can see in the following screenshot:

However, in real life, when we go to a car park, it is easy to see how people park their vehicles in different orientations. To achieve the same result, we can use the **Same rotation** option in Lumion to accomplish that. One way we can do this is by performing the following steps:

1. Select a car and rotate it by 180 degrees.

2. With the initial car selected, hold the *Ctrl* key to select a few more cars.

3. Perform steps 3, 4, and 5 of this recipe to get something like the following screenshot:

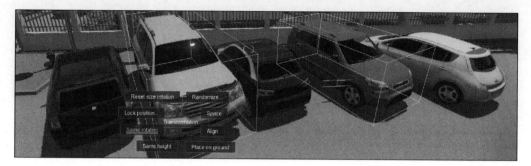

As you can see, now the car park looks more real and believable, and using this recipe has helped us save time and the trouble of manually changing the rotation of every single car or other 3D model. In conclusion, even simple recipes, such as this one, have a significant impact on our project if we know how to use them.

Snapping multiple 3D models

While populating and arranging our project, there are times when a snapping tool comes in handy. We can always use the move and height tools to place the 3D model at the top or next to another 3D model, but Lumion allow us to snap multiple 3D models to the same position in an easy way. Let's see how we can do that in this recipe.

Getting ready

To begin with, you need to have the 3D models placed in the scene and unlocked, and if you are working with different categories, have a look at the *Selecting different categories* recipe in this chapter.

How to do it...

To snap multiple 3D models to the same position, perform the following steps:

1. Press and hold the *Ctrl* key and use the left mouse button to select the 3D models.

2. Select the **Context** menu and select the object that is in the correct position. In the example used in the screenshot, we need to select the planter because we want to align the bush.

3. Select the **Transformation...** submenu and click on the **Align** option, as you can see in the following screenshot:

4. After that, you may need to adjust the height or the rotation of some 3D models.

There's more...

Certainly, we can achieve the same result by using the move option and adjusting the model in place. However, the option of snapping different 3D models is particularly useful in situations when we need to place plants in tight spaces. It helps us avoid the need to move the camera around the 3D model to check whether it is in the right place.

Randomizing 3D models' orientation

While placing content in our project, we are usually concerned about the location of the 3D model. However, later we realize that our project is too uniform, and this is easily spotted with plants, trees, flowers, and other objects. Instead of selecting an individual 3D model and manually rotating, relocating, and rescaling it to bring some variety to our project, Lumion helps us out with a fantastic feature to randomize the orientation, position, and scale of the 3D models.

Getting ready

Before we start, the 3D models need to be already placed in the scene because this feature can be used only for the content that is already present in our project and not while we are newly placing the 3D models.

How to do it...

To randomize the orientation of multiple 3D models, perform the following steps:

1. On the left-hand side of the screen, select the **Objects** menu.
2. Press and hold the *Ctrl* key and drag with the left mouse button to select multiple 3D models.
3. Click on the **Context** menu and select a 3D model.
4. Select the **Transformation...** submenu and then the **Randomize...** option.

5. We can use three options, as shown in the following screenshot:

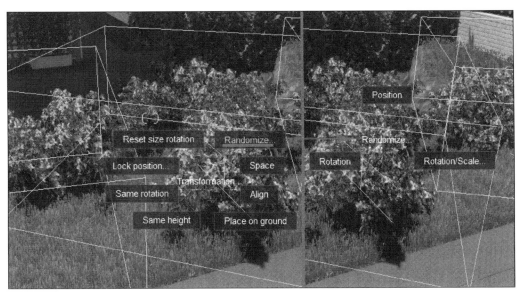

6. Select the **Rotation** option to randomize the orientation of the 3D models selected.

7. Select the **Position** option to randomize the position of the 3D models.

8. Select the the **Rotation/Scale...** option to randomize the orientation and the scale of the 3D models. This options opens another submenu where we can select the percentage of the scale.

There's more...

This is a fantastic feature that really helps us enhance our project with diversity. Randomizing the rotation and the scale are the main aspects, and by using this feature, we can avoid the trouble of pressing the *Z* key every time we place a 3D model to change the size. However, when we randomize the position, this can be a little bit tricky because we cannot control the area where the 3D models are randomized.

Rotate on model

Even in the most perfect project, we can find variations in the terrains and in the building, it's natural that we find inclined surfaces. Rotate on model is a feature in Lumion that allows us to snap to the surface of other 3D models when we are moving a 3D model. We can use this to adjust a car on a slope or a book on a chair. Let's see how.

Getting ready

Before we start, we need to have the 3D model already placed in the scene. This feature will not work while we are newly placing the 3D models.

How to do it...

1. Select the **Objects** menu in the left-hand side of the screen.

2. Select the correct category of the 3D model you want to move; in the screenshot, we have a book that we placed previously.

3. Press the *M* key to move or click on the **Move object** tool that you find in the menu.

4. Move the 3D model and press the *F* key to snap the object to a surface, as you can see in the following screenshot:

If you want to reset the orientation of the 3D model to the original later on, perform the following steps:

1. Click on the **Context** menu button and select the 3D model.

2. Choose the **Transformation...** submenu and click on the **Reset size rotation** button to reset the 3D model to its original orientation.

There's more...

This is a time saver while we are adjusting our project because we avoid losing time trying to do some small adjustments using the rotation tool. We can apply this recipe in several situations. However, once you snap the 3D model to a surface, if you move that 3D model again, and you try to press the *F* key, it doesn't work sometimes. That is why the second part of the recipe is useful.

Constraining the 3D model's rotation

While changing the 3D model's rotation, we can see that when the 3D model is getting closer to the 90 degree angle, it will snap automatically. This is fine, perhaps, in most cases, but there are times when we need to do some precise adjustments and this option can be helpful in our way. Let's see how we can deactivate this feature temporarily.

Getting ready

Before we start, make sure that the 3D model is unlocked.

How to do it...

To turn the snapping 90 degrees option on and off, perform the following steps:

1. Select the **Rotate heading** tool or press the *R* key.

2. Select the object and start rotating the 3D model.

3. The rotation will snap at every 90 degrees or to the cardinal poles, as you can see in the following screenshot:

4. To avoid this snapping, press the *Shift* key once to turn off this option.

5. Rotate the 3D model and you will see that there is no snapping.

6. Press the *Shift* key again if you want to active the 90 degrees snapping option.

4
Constructing Your World

In this chapter, we will cover the following recipes:

- ▶ Shaping the terrain
- ▶ Configuring the terrain brushes
- ▶ Working with the Terrain menu
- ▶ Changing the landscape
- ▶ Painting the landscape
- ▶ Blending the 3D model with the terrain
- ▶ Working with heightmaps
- ▶ Adding water in Lumion
- ▶ Creating a seashore

Introduction

The landscape, where a building is implanted, makes all the difference in any project. It's true that in most cases, the terrain is dug and molded to accommodate the future building; in some circumstances, the architect wants to take benefit of specific characteristics of the terrain. A good example is the Kaufmann Residence designed by Frank Lloyd Wright in 1935, also known as the Fallingwater, and this was designed in a way that it blends with the environment.

Lumion provides tools that are essential to mold and shape the terrain in the best and simplest way possible. In this chapter, we are going to use these tools and see how we can sculpt the terrain and change the landscape characteristics; then, we'll go a little bit further and use some advanced tools, such as heightmaps, to create the terrain in seconds in Lumion.

Shaping the terrain

An initial tactic to sculpt and shape the terrain is to use the terrain brushes available with Lumion. Lumion is not an application like ZBrush, but it does well with the brushes provided to sculpt the terrain, and they are not difficult to master. This recipe is going to explain how we can use them and some practical applications in real projects.

Getting ready

To start, you may want to use a proxy of your building as a reference in the scene and focus your attention on the terrain. A proxy can be just a box with the house dimensions that will work as a visual aid to shape the terrain before importing the final 3D model.

How to do it...

To start sculpting the terrain in your project, perform the following steps:

1. On the left-hand side of the screen, select the **Landscape** menu.

2. This will give you access to a series of tools, as you can see in the following screenshot:

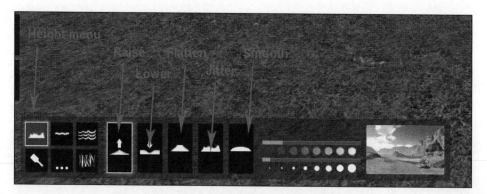

3. There are some additional submenus that allow you to change and create other elements for your project, but we are going to focus our attention on the first menu, the **Height menu**.

4. You can see five rectangular buttons that represent the different brushes we can use to change the terrain.

5. Select the first option, the **Raise** brush.

6. Pressing the left mouse button, drag it onto your terrain to start adding small hills.

7. Click on the **Undo** button if you want to undo your last action, but remember you can go back only once. However, nothing is lost because we can use the **Lower** brush.

8. Select the **Lower** brush and repeat step 6, and now you are sculpting a small valley or lowering the terrain. The next brush helps you to flatten the terrain.

9. Select the **Flatten** brush.

10. This brush, as the name indicates, flattens the terrain if you have a hill or a valley and can be used to create, for example, a flat surface to create a road.

11. The next brush is the **Jitter** brush, and we can say that this brush is a combination of the **Raise** and **Lower** brushes.

12. By pressing the left mouse button, you will see that this brush starts to lower and raise the terrain.

13. Keep the left mouse button pressed and it will eventually create a terrain that looks like a mountain.

14. Let's leave the changes made by the **Jitter** brush as is; we are going to use the last brush available.

15. Select the **Smooth** brush.

16. Use this brush to slowly smooth the hard edges of the terrain, but this is not the same as using the **Flatten** brush.

How it works...

This is just a small overview of the five brush tools that we can find in Lumion. The final result depends on your capability to use these brushes and whether you are using the mouse or a graphic tablet to sculpt the terrain.

We don't need to buy a graphic tablet specifically to work with Lumion, but if you have one and you want to use it to sculpt the terrain, you need to activate the **Toggle Tablet Input** option. To do this, you need to go to the **Settings** menu and select the **Toggle Tablet Input** option that is represented by the icon shown in the following screenshot:

With the tablet input, it is possible to use pen pressure to sculpt the terrain and have more control over the final result. It is not something essential, but can help us speed up the shaping process.

There's more...

Sculpting the terrain is a mix between using these five brushes and using the camera to check the terrain. Depending on the final output, if presented as some still images or a video, it is useful to plan ahead what we need for our project.

With the main building placed, we can save the camera viewpoints that later can be used to check whether the terrain is on the right track. So, before we start with any form of sculpting, it will be good if we take some time and define some camera viewpoints that will be used to produce a still image or a video; also, we can go back and forward using the camera shortcuts to check the terrain while sculpting.

See also

  ▸   To help you control the camera, check the *Navigating in Lumion* recipe in *Chapter 1, Importing in Lumion*

  ▸   To see how you can change the landscape's textures, see the *Painting the landscape* recipe in this chapter

Configuring the terrain brushes

In the *Shaping the terrain* recipe, we saw how to use the five brushes to sculpt the terrain and the different results of each one of them. However, we are not limited to the standard values used in each brush because Lumion allows us to change two settings to help us sculpt the terrain. This control is useful when we need to add details at a small or large scale.

Getting ready

Use a proxy of your building as a reference in the scene so that you can focus your attention just on the terrain.

How to do it...

Adjusting the settings of each brush is really easy; you just need to perform the following steps:

1. Select the **Landscape** menu to activate the **Height menu** with the brushes.
2. For this tutorial, select the **Raise** brush.
3. Next to the brush icons, you can find the **Brush Speed** and **Brush Size** values used, as you can see in the following screenshot:

4. The top bar is the brush speed and the bottom bar is the brush size.
5. Each bar allows you to make accurate adjustments to the settings, and you can use the *Shift* key while dragging with the left mouse button to slowly change the values.
6. The **Brush Speed** setting controls the speed or the time you need to keep the left mouse button pressed so that the brush takes effect.

7. Select the **Raise** brush and click on your terrain with the left mouse button; by doing this, you will see that the longer you leave the button pressed, the bigger will be the amount of terrain you raise.

8. The **Brush Size** setting is self-explanatory; it makes the brush bigger or smaller; a smaller size is not particularly small but when combined with the **Brush Speed** setting, it allows you to make minute adjustments.

How it works...

Lumion doesn't store any values while using these brushes. As an example, this means that the adjustment you make in the **Raise** brush settings will not be applicable when you select the **Lower** brush.

There's more...

Learning how to use these settings will help you take the best from the brushes available; however, there is one brush in particular that will become very useful if you adjust the brush speed and size settings. The **Jitter** brush initially may appear impractical to any project, but this brush can be used to add small variations to the terrain. Using a bigger brush size and by lowering the speed, we can add nice detail to the terrain, and this will help you to create something more interesting than a flat terrain.

See also

▶ To learn more about how to control the terrain, check the *Shaping the terrain* recipe in this chapter

Working with the Terrain menu

Some projects don't require any specific terrain from us, but at the same time, we don't want to use a flat terrain. In the **Terrain** menu, we can find some tools that help us to quickly create mountains and modify other characteristics of our project. Let's see how we can use this menu.

Getting ready

Again, it can be useful to use a proxy of your building before changing the terrain.

How to do it...

Let's explore the **Terrain** menu and some tools that we can find inside it with the following steps:

1. On the left-hand side of the screen, select the **Landscape** menu.

2. By default, the **Height** submenu is selected and is represented by the icon with a mountain profile.

3. Select the **Terrain** submenu that is represented by the icon with three dots, as you can see in the following screenshot:

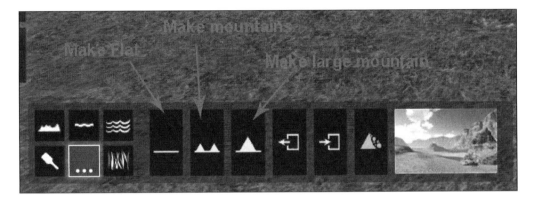

4. Now we have access to several tools to shape the look of the terrain.

5. The first tool is the **Make Flat** tool that will flatten the entire surface of the terrain and delete any hills or valleys you may have.

6. Then we have the **Make mountains** tool. When you click on this button, Lumion generates an interesting-looking terrain with mountains.

7. The next tool is the **Make large mountain** tool that creates, you are right, a big and large mountain in the middle of your scene; all your scenes need to be around this mountain because it is easier to control the place from where the mountain is inserted.

8. You don't have to halt here because you can go back to the **Height** submenu and sculpt what Lumion has created with these tools.

There's more...

There are numerous applications in this menu that we can use while working on a project. For example, we may use the **Height** menu to carve the terrain and get to a point where we feel that the best thing to do is to start from scratch. The **Make Flat** option is the best technique to do this because with just one click, you can get a plane terrain.

Similarly, when working on a project where there are no restrictions with the terrain, I use the **Make mountains** option to start and go to the **Height** menu and change the terrain where I need. The **Terrain** menu, as you can see, has a few more possibilities that can improve the project you are working on, and they are covered later in this chapter.

Changing the landscape

When we start a new project in Lumion, we can start using nine different presets. They sort of work as a shortcut to help us get the appearance we want for our project. Most of the time, we may use the **Grass** preset, but that doesn't mean we get stuck with the landscape presented. In the previous recipes, we saw how we can sculpt the terrain, but we can do more than that in Lumion. Let's have a look and see how we can completely change the aspect of the landscape.

Getting ready

For this tutorial, there is nothing special you need. Save the project just in case you need to reverse the changes.

How to do it...

1. On the left-hand side of the screen, select the **Landscape** menu and click on the **Terrain** submenu button.

2. If your terrain is a plane, you may not notice all the variations; therefore, if you want to see how the landscape is affected, click on the **Make large mountain** option.

3. On the right-hand side of the **Terrain** submenu is the **Choose Landscape** button; it is the one with a thumbnail with a picture of some mountains.

4. Click on this thumbnail and a window appears, as you can see in the following screenshot:

5. You can choose from the 20 presets that will transform your project into a desert and the next moment you are on the high mountains.

6. Choose one preset for your project; this will close the window and take you back to the **Build** mode.

7. If you have hills or valleys, you can verify that now, as you have different materials applied to the ground and rocks. If you have a flat terrain, probably you will not see many changes.

8. On the left-hand side of the **Choose Landscape** button, you will find the **Toggle rock** button.

9. Click on this button to turn off/on the rock material in your landscape.

There's more...

We need to mention that this window with different presets to change the landscape is also present in the **Height** menu.

See also

▶   If you need to change the terrain in order to check the landscape, have a look at the *Shaping the terrain* recipe in this chapter

Painting the landscape

Although we have 20 presets to entirely change the look of the landscape, this doesn't mean that we cannot change any settings and actually paint the landscape. This recipe explores the **Paint** submenu and shows how we can use Lumion's textures to paint and change the landscape completely.

Getting ready

Use a proxy of your building as a reference in the scene so that you can focus your attention just on the terrain.

How to do it...

To start painting the landscape in your project, perform the following steps:

1.   Select the **Landscape** menu on the left-hand side of the screen.
2.   Select the **Paint** submenu, the one with a brush as an icon.
3.   The following screenshot is the menu that appears:

4.   With the left mouse button pressed, you can start painting the terrain.
5.   Each square represents the different materials in the landscape, but you will not see them if you are using a flat terrain.

6. On top of each thumbnail is the **Edit Type** button, which is characterized by a small arrow icon.

7. Click on one of the arrows to change the material and a window will open showing the 42 different materials that are accessible, as shown in the following screenshot:

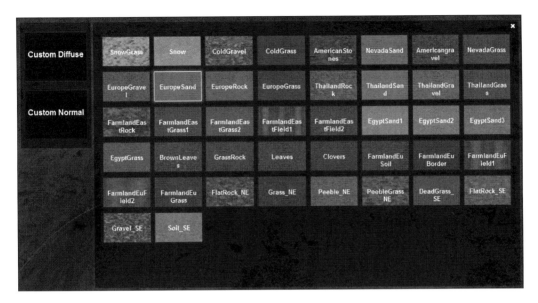

8. To use a texture that you created, click on the **Custom Diffuse** button to upload one texture as a diffuse, and use the **Custom Normal** button to upload a texture to create a bump effect.

9. Select one square to start painting the terrain and use the left mouse button as a brush.

10. Next to the thumbnails, you can find the settings to control the brush speed and the brush size, like the ones you can find in the **Height** submenu.

11. The top bar controls the tile size, and these settings control how big will be the texture used in the material for your terrain.

There's more...

As mentioned, we can change the material used of each element by importing a texture, but remember that you can only import images with the extensions BMP, JPG, TGA, DDS, PNG, PSD, and TIFF. Another point is that we need an image with a good resolution, and it should be seamless to be used in Lumion.

Blending the 3D model with the terrain

Perhaps you don't want the trouble of sculpting the terrain using the tools offered in Lumion. Truth be told, in some situations, it is easier and more productive to model the terrain outside Lumion and import that terrain along with the building. Lumion has fantastic material that blends the terrain we imported with the landscape.

Getting ready

Before you begin, it is essential that you model a terrain in your favorite 3D modeling package and import it in Lumion.

How to do it...

1. Select the **Import** menu.

2. Select the **Edit Materials** button and click on the 3D model you imported.

3. Click on the **Add Material** button to add a new material.

4. After selecting the 3D model, you need to pick the **Landscape** material found in the **Custom** section, as you can see in the following screenshot:

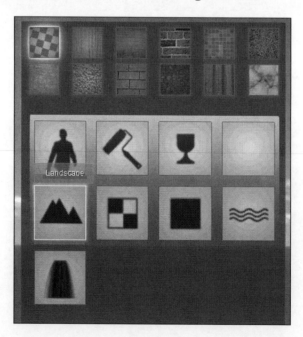

5. Apply this material, and the terrain you just modeled will look like part of the Lumion terrain.

6. You can select the **Paint** submenu and paint on top of this material by adding a different material; when you change the landscape, the material will be updated.

There's more...

Personally, I use this option with the terrain next to the building because I have more control over the way the building works with the terrain. In Lumion, we can use the brushes that are accessible to work with the terrain and compose the scene. This is especially beneficial when we need to work with swimming pools on the ground, and because the brushes to sculpt the terrain only have a circular shape, it is really difficult to create a hole in the ground to accommodate the swimming pool.

Working with heightmaps

Another solution to create accurate terrains is by means of a heightmap. A heightmap is a texture with stored values that can be used, in this case, by Lumion that translates this 2D information into a 3D terrain. This recipe will help you to see how you can import a heightmap and save the terrain you created in Lumion as a heightmap file.

Getting ready

To start, you need to have your heightmap ready, and this texture needs to be saved as a DDS file.

How to do it...

To work with heightmaps in Lumion, perform the following steps:

1. On the left-hand side of the screen, select the **Landscape** menu and click on the **Terrain** submenu button.

2.   The buttons we want to focus our attention on are shown in the following screenshot:

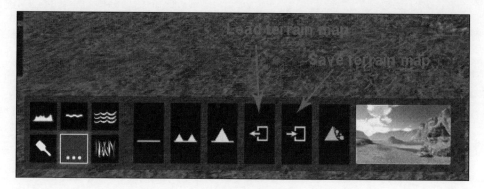

3.   Select the first button to import your heightmap file.

4.   As soon as you import the texture, you will realize that Lumion translated the 2D information into 3D.

5.   Select the second button if you want to export the terrain you created in Lumion and save it for future uses.

How it works...

Lumion has some limitations when using heightmaps. The editable part of the terrain is only a square of 2048 m x 2048 m. Also keep in mind that the heightmap will be stretched to the fullest extent of the square. This means that if you create a texture with 1024 m x 1024 m, once you import it in Lumion, the heightmap is stretched to cover an area of 2048 m x 2048 m.

A heightmap looks something like the following screenshot:

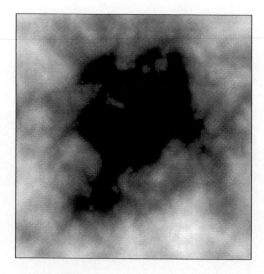

100 percent black is equal to a terrain height of 0 m, and 100 percent white is equal to a terrain height of 200 m. Then, between the black and white, we have 254 scales of gray that can be used to achieve different heights.

There's more...

How can we create a heightmap? A heightmap can be created by hand with Gimp and Photoshop or with a terrain editor. These editors visualize the terrain in 3D and allow you to modify the surface; however, if you want to open a heightmap exported from Lumion, we need to install a plugin to do so using Photoshop or Gimp.

> Download NVIDIA texture tools for Adobe Photoshop from `https://developer.nvidia.com/nvidia-texture-toolsadobe-photoshop`.
>
> Download the GIMP DDS plugin from `https://code.google.com/p/gimp-dds/`.

If you want to use Gimp or Photoshop to manually create the heightmap, start with a black texture and then use really small increments of gray. To help provide some variety to your terrain, try using different brush types and play with the opacity too. Save the texture as a 32-bit DDS heightmap in the `32f` format.

Now, what if I told you that you can create a heightmap of any location on the planet? USGS is a scientific agency of the United States government, and they provide Global Data Explorer.

> You can find Global Data Explorer at `http://gdex.cr.usgs.gov/gdex/`.

With Global Data Explorer, you have access to any part of the world. To use this information in Lumion, you need to select the ASTER data and export the image as GeoTIFF or any other grayscale image; however, of course, you can only use a 2 km x 2 km terrain area in Lumion.

Adding water in Lumion

About 70 percent of the earth's surface is covered by water, and Lumion has some fantastic tools to create beautiful and realistic water surfaces. This recipe can be divided into two parts because we are going to see how we can apply a body of water directly and also use the water material.

Getting ready

If you want to apply the water material to your scene, it is essential that you create a surface and apply a unique material before you export the 3D model to be used in Lumion.

How to do it...

First, let's start by adding a water body to the project with the following steps:

1. Select the **Landscape** menu.
2. Click on the **Water** submenu and the menu appears, as shown in the following screenshot:

3. You can change the look of the water using the **Type** button.
4. Select the **Place object** button to place this body of water.
5. This will create a square that we can control using the icons on each corner to change the size and height.
6. You can change the look of the water by selecting another type of water, but if you have more than two or more bodies of water, they are changed equally.

We can use this option to create a swimming pool, but instead we can make use of the **Water** material by performing the following steps:

1. Select the **Import** menu.
2. Click on the **Edit Materials** button and select the 3D model surface assigned to receive this water material.

3. Select the **Water** material that you can find in the **Custom** menu, as you can see in the following screenshot:

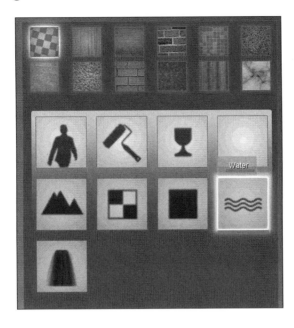

4. Click on the **Ok** button to apply and save the material.

5. Now you have one of Lumion's best materials with fantastic and realistic reflections.

Creating a seashore

Lumion wouldn't be complete without an option to create an ocean. This is one of the best tools available in Lumion because literally in seconds you can create an amazing realistic ocean. Let's see how we can do that.

Getting ready

Make sure that you have a 3D model with good height; otherwise, your house will be under water.

How to do it...

1. Select the **Landscape** menu.

2. Click on the **Ocean** submenu.

3. To create an ocean, click on the ocean on/off button and the menu shown in the following screenshot appears:

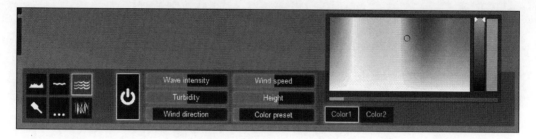

4. Now, you have access to several settings to change the look of the ocean.

5. You can create a calm and relaxing sea or change the sea so drastically that it will look like a storm.

6. Use the **Height** value if you need to adjust the height of the sea; however, keep in mind that the ocean will cover the entire landscape, so you don't have control over the location of the ocean.

5

Controlling the Weather

In this chapter, we will cover the following topics:

- ▶ Defining the sun's direction
- ▶ Modifying the sun's settings
- ▶ Tweaking the shadows
- ▶ Tuning the skylight
- ▶ Adding soft shadows
- ▶ Configuring the Global Illumination effect
- ▶ Modifying and animating the clouds
- ▶ Setting up fog
- ▶ Making it rain and snow
- ▶ Controlling the wind
- ▶ Using the Sun study effect

Introduction

The 3D models, the main construction and the landscape are without any doubt the significant aspects to produce a stunning and eye-catching image or video. These elements help bring out variety and diversity in your project; an additional and important ingredient is climate and the way it can contribute to the atmosphere of the whole project. In Lumion, we can accomplish that using the weather system, which includes the Sun, sky, shadows, and other elements.

This is a further stage in the production process that requires patience to tweak and check the settings, and in Lumion, we have a fair amount of control over almost every single feature. This chapter is aimed at introducing you to some of these settings to produce different moods and environments.

Defining the sun's direction

It is remarkable how little things, such as defining the Sun's direction, have the most considerable amount of impact on a project. Throughout the production process, we may need to adjust the Sun's direction to have a clear view of the project; however, in due course, we will get to a point where we will need to define the final orientation that we are going to use to produce a still image or a movie.

Getting ready

For this recipe, you need to verify the quality of the 3D model used in the **Build** mode so that you can check the shadows and see how the Sun transforms the environment. You need at least a medium quality editor (press the *F2* key) to see the shadows created by the Sun.

How to do it...

To adjust the Sun's orientation, perform the following steps:

1. On the left-hand side of the screen, select the **Weather** menu.

2. With this menu, different tools will become available, as you can see in the following screenshot:

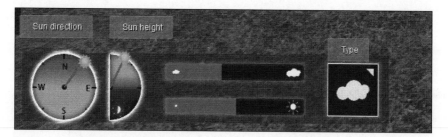

3. For this recipe, we are going to use the first two features.

4. The first is the **Sun direction** feature; with the left mouse button, you can adjust the direction of the Sun.

5. Use the cardinal points to adjust the position of the sun and get the right direction for your project.

6. The second feature is **Sun height**.

7. With the left mouse button, you can adjust the Sun's height; you can see how easy it is to create a sunset scene, night scene, or a midday scene in real time.

There's more...

Perhaps, we could make reference to the fact that there is another setting in the **Weather** menu that has an influence over the Sun. After the **Sun direction** and **Sun height** buttons, we can see the following two bars:

The bottom bar controls the exposure of the Sun's brightness, which indicates that we can modify the Sun's brightness in our 3D world. You may want to use this feature in some situations; so, if required, use the left mouse button to adjust the value. However, keep in mind that this is a very sensible setting and can change the aspect of your scene entirely.

Just to mention that the first bar can be used to control the clouds in the sky.

See also

▶ To have more accurate control over the Sun, check the *Using the Sun study effect* recipe in this chapter

Modifying the sun's settings

Setting up the Sun's direction and height is one of the simplest tasks in Lumion; however, by only using the **Weather** menu, we can start feeling that there is a lack of control over these settings. Fear not though! Lumion offers an effect that provides assistance to control the Sun in a way that can make all the difference when producing a video. This recipe will help you comprehend not only how you can modify the settings for the Sun, but will also provide you with a practical example of how you can apply this recipe in any project.

Getting ready

For this tutorial, we need to move from the **Build** mode to the **Movie** mode, and it is essential that you create a small clip to see the effect.

How to do it...

To modify the Sun's settings, perform the following steps:

1. On the right-hand side of the screen, click on the **Movie** mode button.

2. This will open the movie interface that initially looks like the following screenshot:

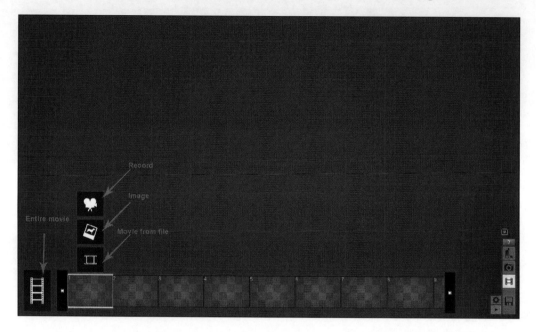

3. If your movie interface is empty, like the one in the previous screenshot, you need to generate a small clip to see the effects.

4. In case you have more than one clip and want to change the Sun's settings, you can pick up one specific clip or the entire movie.

5. On the top-left corner of the screen, click on the **New effect** button, as you can see in the following screenshot:

6. Select the **World** tab and click on the **Sun** effect.

7. After selecting this effect, you should have the following menu on the left-hand side of the movie interface:

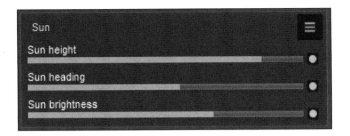

8. From the menu seen in the previous screenshot, you can modify the same options that you can find in the **Weather** menu.

So, what is the point of using this effect to control the Sun? If we look at the preceding screenshot again, we can see the presence of a small dot at the right-hand side of each setting. Let's see how these small dots can help us:

1. Picking up from where we left off, on the bottom of the preview window, you can see a large bar that represents the length of the clip that is selected.

2. With the left mouse button, click-and-drag on the bar to go through the animation; this works like fast-forwarding or rewinding a video.

3. Drag the red bar until the animation starts.

4. In the **Sun** effect, let's use the **Sun height** feature to demonstrate the effect.

5. Move the **Sun height** slider until you get a sunset effect, and click on the small dot on the right-hand side of the bar to create a keyframe.

6. Look at the red bar to see a small line that gets drawn, as exemplified in the following screenshot:

7. Drag the red bar to the end of the clip.

8. In the **Sun** effect, adjust the **Sun height** setting until you get a midday Sun and create another keyframe.

9. Play the clip, and you will find that we animated the Sun, creating the effect of the Sun rising up in the morning and moving across the sky.

10. Getting back to the **Sun** effect, you will see that the menu changes slightly, as you can see in the following screenshot:

11. The keys above the **Sun height** setting allow you to move between the keyframes created, and the small cross deletes the current keyframe.

How it works...

If you have some familiarity with animation, you will understand the concept of using keyframes. With keyframes, we can delineate the starting and ending points of any smooth transition and that is precisely what we did in this recipe.

If we go back to the screenshot with the red bar, we will see that between the keyframes, there is a line that represents the animation between the two values. We defined where the Sun's height started and ended, and Lumion completed the frames between the starting and ending points with a smooth transition. This doesn't mean that we are stuck with just two keyframes; you are free to use as many keyframes as you want to achieve the look you desire.

There's more...

This is a concept that we can easily apply to other effects, and it has the ability to enhance your final output; also, as mentioned before, we can apply this effect to a single clip or an entire movie. However, if you apply, let's say, this **Sun** effect to the entire movie and later on add the same effect to an individual clip, this last action will overwrite the initial effect.

We are not constrained to the **Sun** effect because other effects such as clouds, wind, snow, and many more can be animated. However, to do this, you need time and patience to test and tweak these settings.

See also

▸ To create a small clip, check the *Creating a camera path* recipe in *Chapter 10, Bringing Your World to Life*

Tweaking the shadows

A shadow can be defined as an area that is not or is only partially illuminated because an object is obstructing its source of illumination. It is true that we don't think that shadows are important and essential elements to create a good-looking scenario, but without them our project will be dull. This recipe is going to help us use the **Shadow** effect to tweak and correct the shadows in order to meet our requirements and the finishing look we want to accomplish.

Getting ready

Before we start, it is essential that you have at least a small clip created in the **Movie** mode or an image if you are using the **Photo** mode where we can see the effect.

How to do it...

To tweak the shadows in your scene, perform the following steps:

1. Open the **Photo** or **Movie** mode using the buttons on the right-hand side of the screen.
2. Create a small clip if you are using the **Movie** mode.
3. After selecting the clip on the top-left corner of the screen, click on the **New effect** button.
4. The **World** tab is selected by default.
5. Select the **Shadow** effect.
6. After selecting this effect, you should have the following menu on the left-hand side of the movie interface:

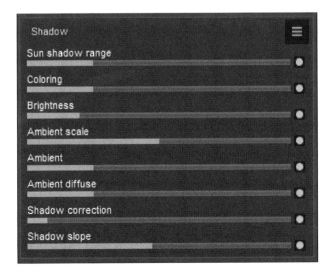

7. This effect permits us to adjust and correct some problems with the shadows in a project.

8. Select the first setting **Sun shadow range** and adjust the value using the slider to increase or decrease the value.

9. Use this setting when you stop seeing the shadows cast by the 3D models in the scene from a certain distance.

10. Let's move to the last two options: **Shadow correction** and **Shadow slope**.

11. These settings are used when you can perceive a gap or an offset between the 3D model and the shadow that is produced, as you can see in the following screenshot:

12. Every project is different, so there are no accurate values to solve this issue. Adjust the **Shadow correction** value to correct the gap between the 3D model and shadow.

13. In some conditions, you can notice leaks of light going through the 3D models; adjust the **Shadow slope** slider to correct this issue.

How it works...

We need to understand the way in which Lumion works with shadows to fully comprehend how we can apply this effect in a precise way. To prevent flickering or any other shadow artifacts, Lumion applies the shadow on top of every surface with an offset. This is more noticeable in interior scenes when the camera is close to the 3D models and they don't look like they are touching the ground. So, we need to apply this effect in our project in order to solve some artifacts that may appear.

There's more...

In the first setting, **Sun shadow range**, we need to balance the value while adjusting the setting. This is because initially we may feel inclined to play safe and increase this setting to its maximum value. However, you will find that when working on small projects if you use a high value, the shadow resolution is not the best one, as you can see in the following screenshot:

This means that we need to balance the value when using this effect because every project is different and we need to take time to check what values are better. In a situation where we are moving from a wide shot and start zooming and performing a close up, don't forget to use the keyframes to animate the transition from a high shadow range value to a lower one.

Tuning the skylight

An additional aspect connected to the shadows in Lumion, and it happens in the real world too, is the influence of the sky over shadows. Taking a look at the shadows in any project, you can easily realize how a sunset or a midday scene can transform the color of the shadow. In this recipe, we will learn how to control and change the influence that skylight has on shadows.

Getting ready

Before you start, you need to have some 3D models in your project to see the effect and make sure that they are at least of medium quality to see the shadows.

How to do it...

To change the effect of the skylight on the shadows, perform the following steps:

1. Change the mode from **Build** to **Photo** or **Movie**.

2. Click on the **New effect** button.

3. From the **World** tab, select the **Shadow** effect.

4. The new effect appears on the left-hand side of the screen and to change the shadow saturation use the **Coloring** value.

5. A value close to **1** will increase the bluish look, while a value lower than this will assign a warmer color to the model, as you can see in the following screenshot:

6. Remember that in the **Movie** mode, you have an option to use this effect in the entire movie or just a small clip.

There's more...

This is an effect that can help us provide an additional touch to the mood we are trying to accomplish. First, I wouldn't advise to entirely remove the effect that the sky has on the shadows; this is what happens in real life, and if this influence is removed completely, you can create a flat movie or image. Second, we can give a warmer or cooler effect to our project by tweaking this setting, and this can work in our favor.

The blue color gives a cooler effect and is often used when working on a winter scene, overcast condition, or early morning; on the other hand, if we need a warmer and sunny scene, it makes sense to remove this bluish tone and use the red and orange colors more.

Adding soft shadows

In the previous recipes, we have been working entirely with hard shadows. The Sun in our 3D world can produce these hard shadows, and they are called by this name because they have strong and well-defined edges with less transition between illumination and the shadow. Soft shadows can be produced by the Sun in certain circumstances, and the sky, likewise, can create these diffused shadows with soft edges. Let's see how we can apply soft shadows to our project and how they can enrich the final look.

Getting ready

Before you start, you need to have some 3D models in your project to see the effect; make sure that these are at least of medium quality so that you can see the shadows. In any case, you can use one of the examples available in the **Examples** tab to see how soft shadows can boost an image or movie.

How to do it...

To add soft shadows to your project, perform the following steps:

1. Select the **Photo** or **Movie** mode.

2. Click on the **New effect** button and from the **World** tab, select the **Shadow** effect.

3. This effect now appears in your interface on the left-hand side, and we are going to focus our attention on the **Ambient scale**, **Ambient**, and **Ambient diffuse** settings, as you can see in the following screenshot:

4. Look for a place in your scene where two surfaces make contact and start adjusting the **Ambient** slider.

5. By increasing the value of the **Ambient** setting, we can see that wherever two surfaces are in contact with each other, a shadow starts to appear. This effect is also known as **Ambient occlusion**.

6. Change the **Ambient** scale if you wish to increase or decrease the size of the occluded area with the soft shadows.

7. The **Ambient diffuse** setting can also be used to darken the occluded area, and this setting can be used along with the **Ambient** setting.

There's more...

Don't overlook what soft shadows can bring to your project. The process of adding soft shadows is often employed to enhance the look of a CG output; however, at the same time, we need to add these types of shadows to our scene in a very subtle way. The following screenshot displays the same scene but only the left-hand side of the screen has the soft shadows enabled:

It makes a big difference when we use soft shadows in any scene. With the correct scale and amount of soft shadows, we can get a pleasing and good-looking project.

Configuring the global illumination

So far, we have been looking at how we can use the **Weather** menu to create an enjoyable environment for our exterior scenes. Lumion is also capable of producing beautiful interior scenes, but we need to work a little bit with the interior illumination before we can produce something that is presentable and eye-catching. For interior scenes, we can use the **Global Illumination** effect to improve the illumination that is either provided by the Sun or some artificial source of illumination. Let's see how we can improve the interior look and illumination using **Global Illumination**.

Getting ready

Before you begin, move the camera to the interior of your building to check and tweak the settings. If you just want to test this effect, use one of the examples that you can find in the **Examples** tab.

How to do it...

To improve the illumination of an interior scene, perform the following steps:

1. Click on the **New effect** button.

2. From the **World** tab, select the **Global Illumination** effect.

3. This effect is added to your scene and the following screenshot shows the default settings:

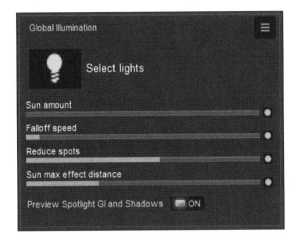

4. When using the Sun as the main source of light, use the **Sun amount** setting to increase the quantity of sunlight that enters and bounces inside the building.

5. The **Falloff speed** setting controls the intensity and needs to be used in conjunction with the **Sun amount** setting.

6. The **Reduce spots** setting helps in removing artifacts that may occur while using this effect with animations in particular.

This primary section is aimed for scenes where the Sun is the main source of light that illuminates the project. However, if we are using artificial light, such as spotlights, we need to perform the following steps:

1. Apply the **Global Illumination** effect to your project.

2. Click on the **Select lights** button to select the spotlights in your scene.

3. This will get you back to the **Build** mode where you need to select the spotlights in use.

4. On the bottom-left corner of the screen, Lumion shows how many spotlights are selected, as you can see in the following screenshot:

5. After selecting the spotlights, you need to increase the **Spotlight GI amount** value to start perceiving the result in your scene.

6. You can use the **Preview Spotlight GI and Shadows** button to check how the **Global Illumination** effect is affecting the scene.

How it works...

Global illumination is meant to add more realistic lighting to 3D scenes. It takes into account not only direct illumination, but also the light rays from the same or other sources that are reflected by the surfaces in the scene, which is called indirect illumination. The icon used to represent the **Global Illumination** effect reflects this idea because we see the Sun and a light ray that is reflected by the surface. This is what happens when we use this effect, and the calculations done by Lumion can greatly improve the look of any interior scene.

There's more...

Even though this recipe is divided in to two sections, one for when we are using the Sun and the other when using spotlights, we can combine both when using the Sun for illumination. This means that we can get good results when the Sun is lighting the scene, and we also pick spotlights to expand the illumination of the interior.

Modifying and animating the clouds

An element that can bring an extra touch to the final movie are the clouds. This is a component that does not always cross our mind when trying to attain a good-looking and realistic movie. Lumion provides us with a lot of freedom not only to change the appearance of the clouds, but also to animate and even create volume clouds to bring this fine-tuning to a different dimension. In this recipe, we are going to look into three different effects and how we can apply them to our project.

Getting ready

Before you begin, you need a simple animation to see these effects in action. If necessary, create a small clip with a few seconds.

How to do it...

Let's start with the **Cloud** effect; to use this effect, perform the following steps:

1. Click on the **New effect** button.

2. Choose the **Weather** tab and select the **Cloud** effect.

3. The following screenshot shows the settings that are available with this effect:

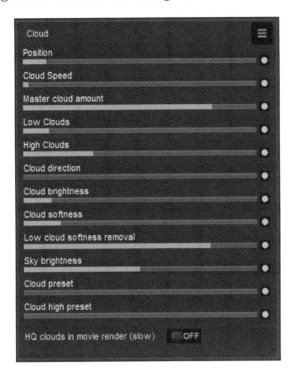

4. Some of the settings are self-explanatory, such as the **Position**, **Cloud Speed**, and **Cloud direction** settings, just to mention a few.

5. Lumion gives you the control of two layers of clouds: the low and high clouds; the amount of both types of clouds are controlled using the **Low Clouds** and **High Clouds** settings.

6. Use the **Master cloud amount** setting to control the amount of both clouds in the project.

7. Change the type of clouds using the presets available. Adjust the **Cloud preset** setting to change the low clouds and the **Cloud high preset** setting to adjust the high clouds.

8. We can use the final setting to improve the look of the clouds in the final movie, but keep in mind that this increases the time it will take to render the movie.

9. The best way of using this effect is by animating the position and speed of the clouds, thus bringing life to your movie.

We can also apply clouds to the horizon using the **Horizon Cloud** effect with the following steps:

1. Click on the **New effect** button.

2. From the **Weather** tab, select the **Horizon Cloud** effect which will add these settings to the movie interface, as shown in the following screenshot:

3. This is quite a simple effect where the **Amount** value defines the amount of clouds on the horizon.

4. The **Type** setting works in a similar way as the preset setting in the previous effect.

5. Adjust the **Softness** setting to change between crispy or wispy clouds.

The final effect that we are going to see adds a special layer of clouds that are volumetric, which means that you can even fly through clouds using this effect. Let's see how we can use the **VolumeClouds** effect with the following steps:

1. Click on the **New effect** button, and from the **Weather** tab, select the **VolumeClouds** effect.

2. The settings that will become available are really similar to some of the previous effects.

3. We want to focus our attention on the second setting, **Height**. This setting allows us to move the clouds up and down in our project, something that is not available in the previously mentioned effects.

4. You can either adjust the **Height** setting or move the camera up and create a beautiful effect like the following screenshot:

There's more...

With these effects, there are nine types of clouds available to use in your project, and to see them, you need to select the **Weather** menu in the **Build** mode and click on the last button called **Type**. This will open a new window where you can see and select one of the nine clouds available. These nine types of clouds are the ones that you can use when you adjust the preset setting.

There is another effect that you can add to the project that works really well with the clouds. Under the **World** tab, you can find the **Contrails** effect that adds the trails of an airplane leaving in the sky.

See also

▶ To have a more accurate control over the Sun, check the *Using the Sun study effect* recipe in this chapter

Setting up fog

Fog is a natural phenomenon that can be added to our project, and it can really change a scene dramatically. With it, we can make a scene more mysterious or reproduce the haze where dust, smoke, and other dry particles obscure the clarity of the sky. With the **Fog** effect, we can achieve this and much more.

Getting ready

Before we start, go to the **Photo** or **Movie** mode in order to apply and see this effect in action.

How to do it...

1. In the **Photo** or **Movie** mode, click on the **New effect** button.

2. Under the **Weather** tab, select the **Fog** effect.

3. When you add this effect to your project, initially you cannot see any change and that is because you need to start tweaking the following settings:

4. Start by increasing the **Fog density** setting, and you will start seeing fog once you get to the **1.5** value.

5. To create the haze effect, you need to adjust the **Fog falloff** setting to a value of over **0.1**.

6. Finally, change the color using the color board, where you can adjust not only the color, but also the intensity of the fog.

There's more...

I use this effect to work on the depth of the compositions. The way we layer the 3D models with the foreground, middle ground, and background forms a very simple rule that creates a depth perception, and the haze effect really helps to separate these elements.

Making it rain and snow

The fact that we can add rain and snow, as easy as reading this sentence, really proves that Lumion is a powerful and versatile application. Adding rain or snow is something that we can easily achieve by adding two effects in the **Photo** or **Movie** mode.

Getting ready

We don't need anything special for this tutorial, just make sure that you have some 3D models in the scene to see how the snow works with the environment.

How to do it...

Let's start by adding rain with the following steps:

1. Click on the **New effect** button, and from the **Weather** tab, select the **Rain** effect.
2. Once you select this effect, your scene changes dramatically into a rainy day.
3. Correct the **Drop distortion** value if the rain in your project looks strange.
4. Adjust the **Cloudy** setting to quickly darken the sky and increase the humidity in the air.
5. The **Wind X** and **Wind Y** settings let you change the direction of the rain.

The next in line is the **Snow** effect and the following steps show how it works:

1. From the **Weather** tab, select the **Snow** effect.
2. Again, your scene changes to a winter look with snow falling around everywhere.
3. Adjust the **Snow density** setting to a lower value if you want your scene with snow on the ground, but without snow falling down.
4. The **Snow layer** setting can really bring your scene to life.
5. Start by increasing the slider to see how all the 3D models in your scene start getting covered by snow.
6. You can animate this setting to give a more realistic impression that snow is falling and covering the environment.

There's more...

A side note when using the **Rain** effect is that when we add this effect to our scene, there is something that is not right and that is the shadows on the ground. With the sky so dark, there are almost no shadows, so we need to correct this error by adding the **Sun** effect and completely removing the **Sun brightness** value.

The same applies to the **Snow** effect. Use the **Sun** effect to remove the shadows, but you can still see a very faded shadow in the snow that really gives you a cool look.

Keep in mind that although this is a great effect, not everything is perfect. Aside from the fact that we need to add the **Sun** effect to remove the shadows, the rain doesn't interact with other water surfaces and the ground doesn't get that wet look. To get the wet look, you need to work with the material settings and increase the reflection.

Controlling the wind

Lumion by default uses wind in any project you start. Once you add the first trees, you can see how they slowly move showing the effect of the wind. We can control the wind using the, yes you are right, the **Foliage Wind** effect.

Getting ready

To see this effect in action, you need to add some plants to your project.

How to do it...

To control the wind in your scene, perform the following steps:

1. In the **Photo** or **Movie** mode, click on the **New effect** button.
2. Select the **Foliage Wind** effect found under the **Weather** tab.
3. You can increase the value to **0.5**, and this will simulate a windy day.
4. Try to use this effect along with the **Rain** effect to create a rainy day look.

Using the Sun study effect

Another option to control the Sun is using a new feature introduced in Lumion: Version 4. This option, that we can find under the **Effects** label, is called **Sun study**. It is an amazing feature that allows us to select any point on the planet and mimic the Sun in that location. However, there is much more that we can do with this effect.

Getting ready

If you want a specific location, find out the latitude and longitude in order to use that location with this effect.

How to do it...

1. With the **Photo** or **Movie** mode enabled, add a new effect.

2. From the **World** tab, select the **Sun study** effect.

3. Once you add this effect to your project, you will notice a subtle change in the environment, and this happens because Lumion uses a default value to place the Sun based on the geo-coordinates and time parameters.

4. Start by changing the location and you can do that by using the last two settings, **Latitude** and **Longitude**, as shown in the following screenshot:

5. An easier way to get the correct location for your project is by using the pin point in the map.

6. Select the button with an icon that looks like a pencil and this opens a new window with the planet earth.

7. To select a new position, use the left mouse button to click-and-drag the planet around.

8. Use the scroll wheel to zoom in to make an accurate selection.

9. After selecting the location, click on the **Back** button to return to the **Photo** or **Movie** mode.

10. To get the best from this effect, you need to try the different settings available.

11. Use the keyframes to animate the Sun in a way that it moves around using the **Hour** or **Minute** setting to create smooth transitions.

There's more...

To use this effect, you need to place the main building with the correct orientation. This means that if the main elevation is facing south in the project, we need to do that in Lumion in order to use this effect. How can we do that? A small trick is using the **Weather** menu. Use the **Sun direction** setting to place the Sun at the correct position. For example, I will adjust the Sun to be at the north, and then I will rotate the 3D model knowing that the Sun is indicating the north.

6
Working with Lumion Materials

In this chapter, we will cover the following recipes:

- ▶ Rolling back materials
- ▶ Configuring materials
- ▶ Making the 3D model invisible
- ▶ Creating a realistic glass
- ▶ Saving materials
- ▶ Streaming water
- ▶ Glowing materials
- ▶ Adding realistic grass
- ▶ Improving reflections
- ▶ Correcting flickering

Introduction

The reaction between light and the surface of an object is what our eyes capture, and the information processed enables us to see and recognize materials. We can effortlessly distinguish whether something is made of wood, metal, stone, or glass. Without light, this isn't possible; nevertheless, the material, which the object is made of, has a key role as well. The material defines how light should act in response to the rays of light that hit the surface. This tiny introduction helps us to understand that when we define materials, we are actually defining how light should react with that specific surface.

Lumion is remarkable in this area too because it offers us more than 500 materials that are ready to be applied in the 3D models we import. We don't need to lose any time tweaking and defining the settings to create beautiful materials. This chapter is aimed not to create materials, but at how we can use some features to take the best from what Lumion offers.

Rolling back materials

This is a very straightforward recipe where we will find out how to go back and reverse any material's application. Technically, there are two ways in which we can do that, and this recipe will help you how to comprehend and also let you know the limitations involved in each option.

Getting ready

To begin, it is essential that you have a 3D model imported in Lumion so that you can add some materials in order to understand this recipe. However, you need to add some different materials to your 3D model while modeling so that Lumion can see the surfaces. This means that if your 3D model has only one material when it is imported in Lumion, you will only be able to add one material. In this case, Lumion doesn't recognize surfaces but recognizes only materials.

How to do it...

Let's start by applying some materials to the 3D model by performing the following steps:

1. From the left-hand side of the screen, select the third menu, the **Import** menu.
2. Select the **Edit materials** button, the one that is represented by the bucket icon.
3. Select the 3D model you imported to your scene to start adding some materials.
4. Click on the **Add material** button and choose a surface/material for your 3D model.
5. Once you choose the material, a new window with all the materials appears on the left-hand side of the screen.
6. It is up to you what materials you want to add, but for demonstration purposes, let's make a mistake and select a wood material.
7. Select the **Wood** tab to open the library that contains the materials, and select any material you want.
8. This will be an error because what we really want is a brick material.
9. You can approach the process of reverting or rolling back to the previous materials in two ways.

10. The most radical way is using the **Cancel changes** button, as you can see in the following screenshot:

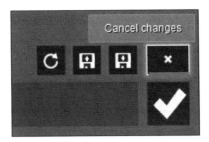

11. Clicking on this button will discard all your changes and take you back to the **Import** menu.

12. This may not be the greatest solution if you only want to revert to the last material and not the whole set of materials applied.

13. To remove a single material, you need to delete it from the slot that is in use; to do this, double-click on the **Delete Material** button, as shown in the following screenshot:

14. After deleting the material, you need to click on the **Add material** button again to add a new material.

In case you need to replace or delete other materials applied to your 3D model, perform the following steps:

1. At the bottom of the screen, there is a bar with small thumbnails that represent the materials present in the 3D model selected.

2. When you hover the mouse over the thumbnail, Lumion highlights where the material is applied, helping you confirm whether you are selecting the right material.

3. Click on the thumbnail and follow steps 11 to 14 mentioned in this recipe.

How it works...

Just a reminder that when we model in 3ds Max, Revit, Maya, or any other application, the materials we use in the 3D model are the main foundation; in Lumion, we have to add materials as well. This means that if you use a single material for the entire 3D model, Lumion recognizes one single material and that is all you can add; consequently, always check whether you have enough materials applied to your 3D model before exporting it to Lumion.

There's more...

What about assigning a name for each material? Well, that needs to be defined in the 3D modeling package because the name you assign to the 3D model is the name that Lumion is going to use. In plain English, prior to exporting the 3D model, you need to take some time and rename the materials in use because something like `Material_37_copy` is not going to help you later on when you have, perhaps, more than 15 materials in your scene, and you are trying to figure out what `Material_37_copy` is supposed to be.

Configuring materials

As mentioned, Lumion has more than 500 materials on hand and generally this is more than adequate. Still, Lumion is a very flexible application, and for this reason, you are not fixed with just these materials. We have the opportunity to use our own textures to create other materials. This recipe is not going to show you all the settings that you can use to tweak the material; instead, we are going to focus on how we can replace and adjust an outside texture.

Getting ready

To begin, it is essential that you have a 3D model imported in Lumion so that you can add some materials, and don't forget to have some textures ready to be applied to the model.

Also, you need two types of textures. The first one is called **Diffuse**, and in plain English, it is the image file with color information; the second one is called **Normalmap**, and you will recognize them as these textures have a purple/blue color. Both the images shown in the following screenshot give you an idea of what you need:

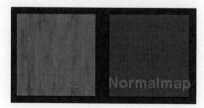

How to do it...

To build a material in your project, perform the following steps:

1. From the left-hand side of the screen, select the third menu: the **Import** menu.

2. Select the **Edit materials** button.

3. Choose the 3D model you imported and click on the **Add material** button.

4. To start a new material, you need to use the **Standard** material that you can find in the **Custom** menu, which looks like the following screenshot:

5. Select this material to begin using your own textures and to modify some properties.

6. The next step is loading the images or textures you want to use on this particular surface; to do this, use the third button called **Textures**, and you will be presented with two blank thumbnails, as shown in the following screenshot:

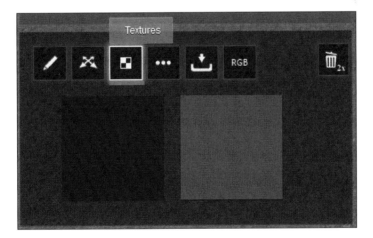

7. Using this panel, you will be able to import a new texture or replace the one in use.

8. Click on the **Change Diffuse texture** option to add the **Diffuse** texture, and a new window becomes visible through which you can navigate to the folder that contains the texture you desire.

9. Repeat the same step for the **Normalmap** texture.

10. Let's pause here to bring out another point that you may find practical. Even though with some 3D modeling packages it isn't essential, you can technically import UVs along with the 3D model.

 UV mapping refers to the way in which each 3D surface is mapped to a 2D texture. This means that if you have UVs on the surface, you can have an accurate control of how the texture is presented on that surface.

In order to make use of any UV mapping that you have done in your preferred 3D modeling package, you need to perform the following steps:

1. Follow all the previous steps and select the first button called **Properties**, as shown in the following screenshot:

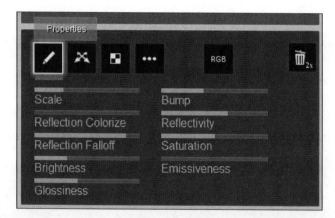

2. You need to change the value in the **Scale** setting to **0**, as shown in the previous screenshot.

3. When you remove the **Scale** option entirely, Lumion assumes that you want to use the UV mapping imported with the 3D model.

How it works...

The **Standard** material is not only intended to create a material from scratch. The materials you import along with the 3D model can be modified by means of this material; this helps to improve the bump effect, adjustment of the reflection, and clip surfaces, just to mention a few.

There's more...

In some circumstances, I like to use a shortcut to swiftly create materials using my own textures. Let's say that we are working on the exterior walls, and the material for these walls are bricks and I have those textures ready to use. Normally, we assign a **Standard** material, and then from there, we import the textures and start adjusting different properties to get the correct settings. If you are in a rush, instead of assigning a **Standard** material, just select a brick material from the Lumion library and replace the textures using the ones you have available, avoiding any adjustments.

Making the 3D model invisible

Making a 3D model invisible or hiding surfaces from our 3D model is something that we don't anticipate to do in every project. However, there are times when the **Invisible** material can be very handy, and this recipe demonstrates not only where to find this material and how to apply it, but also some specific situations that we may consider while using this material.

Getting ready

To begin, it is vital that you have a 3D model imported in Lumion so that you can add some materials in order to understand this recipe. On the other hand, if you don't have any 3D model available, just use one of the scenes that you can find in the **Examples** tab.

How to do it...

To make a surface invisible in Lumion, you need to perform the following steps:

1. From the left-hand side of the screen, select the third menu, the **Import** menu.
2. Select the **Edit materials** button and the 3D model you imported.
3. Click on the **Add material** button and choose a surface for your 3D model.

4. Select the **Invisible** material, which is in fact invisible, as you can see in the following screenshot:

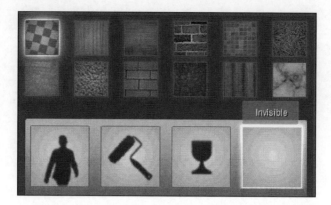

5. After selecting this material, you will notice that the surface apparently vanishes and is no longer used by Lumion to calculate any shadows or collisions.

6. Click on the **OK** button to confirm and save this material.

There's more...

You may be scratching your head thinking, "How on earth is this material helpful?" Personally, I use this material in two situations, but let me tell you that this not something that you can use in every single project.

The first condition is really obvious and is involved when you need to delete a section from the 3D model that for the time being is no longer essential. It is true that you can reload the 3D model with the changes, but in some cases, this is the easiest way to remove it.

The second situation where this material is particularly useful is when you prepare the camera for rendering. Let me explain. In interior scenes, it can be difficult to place the camera in a position that gives us plenty of room to work. Sometimes, to capture the full picture, we need to place the camera in a location that can intersect with some geometry. This is the time when the **Invisible** material is really useful and can save us the trouble of going back and perhaps adjusting the geometry.

Creating a realistic glass

Glass is essential in any project we work. From the glass in a complex window to a simple cup made of glass, this material has a deep impact on a still image and even more on a movie, helping us capture the light and reflections of the environment. Lumion has a glass material that can be used to create some of these materials. Let's see how we can manipulate the **Glass** material to get a more realistic look.

Getting ready

To begin with this recipe, you need some surfaces to apply this **Glass** material and some textures to use as an example.

How to do it...

To apply a glass to your scene, perform the following steps:

1. From the left-hand side of the screen, select the third menu, the **Import** menu.

2. Select the **Edit materials** button and click on the **Add material** button.

3. From the **Custom** library, select the **Glass** material that you can find next to the **Invisible** material.

4. As soon as you have this material, the surface selected is transformed to a transparent and almost invisible surface.

5. The settings used for this material tend to be the best in most cases, but you can adjust the **Reflectivity**, **Glossiness**, and **Minimum reflection** settings to get the best result for your scene.

6. To tint the glass with a different color, click on the **Color** button and select a color.

7. Tweak the **Transparency** setting to create a more opaque material.

8. If you adjust both the **Transparency** and **Reflectivity** settings, you can create a translucent material.

Before we jump on to the next recipe, thinking that this is all we can do with the **Glass** material, let me tell you that we can use textures with it using the **Texture Influence** setting to create some nice effects on the surface of the glass; we can do this by performing the following steps:

1. Follow steps 1 and 2 of the initial recipe.

2. Select the material with a texture that was exported along with the 3D model. This will not work with Lumion materials.

3. Select the **Glass** material, and once more the surface becomes transparent, reflecting the 3D world.

4. Reduce the **Transparency** setting to something like **0.6**.

5. Increase the **Texture Influence** value until you start to see the texture again.

6. In this example, I get something like the following screenshot:

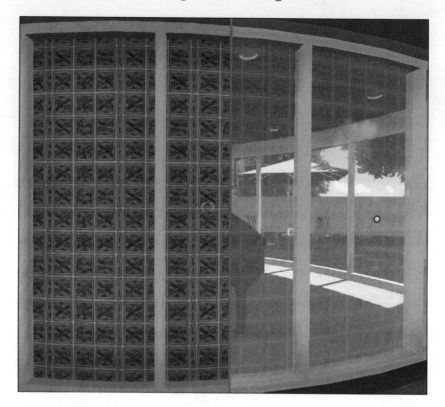

7. You can increase the **Texture Influence** value to **1** and use the **Transparency** setting to configure this outcome.

The **Glass** material can add a nice touch to the scene, but perhaps, this is not exactly what we are looking for in an exterior project where we want to add some highly reflective surfaces without transparency. I recommend that you have a look at the *Improving reflections* recipe in this chapter for some tips to create highly reflective surfaces.

How it works...

A simple explanation could be this: Lumion knew that before we applied the **Glass** material, there was already a material with a texture; as a result, when we reduced the transparency and started cranking up the **Texture Influence** setting, Lumion knew that it needed to use the texture that was previously assigned to that surface. However, this is possible only when you export the 3D model with the material on the surface that already has a texture assigned. As mentioned before, this will not work with other Lumion materials. Also, the effect we get using the **Texture Influence** setting is more noticeable if you use a black and white texture.

There's more...

Doubled sided is another option that can be used when we apply the **Glass** material to a surface with two materials. Some applications such as SketchUp let you apply a material on one side of the surface and a totally different material on the other side. Lumion works with a single-faced surface, but with the **Glass** material, we can bypass this restriction.

Getting back to the effect we get using the **Texture Influence** setting, we may not see a functional application for this feature. However, this option comes in handy in several situations. First, it can be used to add amazing details to objects that use glass, and this can be used with tables, bowls, ornaments, and other 3D models with glass.

The second way we can apply this feature is by faking the grilles and the interior details of a window. Why would we want to do that? Well, when working on a project, where a building is put up in an urban environment, this is a great way to add an extra touch to the surrounding buildings without having to model extra detail.

This feature is incredibly useful when creating these types of scenes because by using an image, as shown in the following screenshot, you can add details that otherwise will consume time and resources to produce:

Saving materials

During the production, it is expected that we save the materials applied to the 3D models. This should be done for precaution purposes, in case something goes wrong or when we need to go back and forth with materials, without having to lose any settings. Lumion has an option to save the materials you applied to a 3D model and later on load them again, if necessary. There is another feature that this recipe is going to show you which will give you a chance to save a single material instead of material sets. Let's see how we can use both of these options.

Getting ready

To use this recipe, you need some 3D models in your project to apply the materials and save them.

How to do it...

To save a material set, perform the following steps:

1. From the left-hand side of the screen, select the third menu, the **Import** menu.
2. Select the **Edit materials** button.
3. Select the 3D model and apply some materials in case you don't have any.
4. On the right-hand side of the screen, you can see a number of buttons; to save this material set, click on the third button called **Save material set**, as you can see in the following screenshot:

5. A new window will open and you can save this material set by giving it a name and clicking on the **Save** button.
6. This saves a file with the extension .mtt that stands for **Material list** which we can load later to restore the material.
7. To load this file, you need to click on the second button called **Load material set**.
8. Again, a window will open and you need to select the file that you saved previously and then click on **Open**.
9. Subsequent to Lumion loading the file, another window will be presented that will give you the opportunity to choose which materials need to be overwritten.
10. Click on the thumbnails that represent the different materials to select or deselect the materials.
11. After this, click on the **Overwrite materials** button and the materials you selected are applied to the 3D model.

Undoubtedly, this is something useful but is very restricted. The save and load material sets options will only work if you use the same 3D model because you cannot load a material set in a totally different 3D model. There is nothing we can do if we use the default Lumion materials, but this changes when we apply the **Standard** materials. Let's see how we can save and load individual materials by performing the following steps:

1. Apply a **Standard** material to your 3D model.

2. After making the required adjustments, click on the **Copy and Save** button, as you can see in the following screenshot:

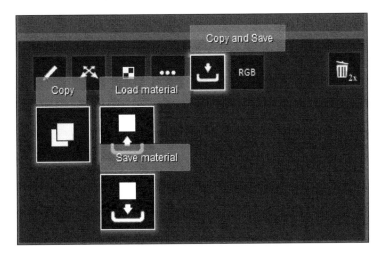

3. Click on the **Copy** button to copy all the settings, and the fourth button called **Paste** appears.

4. Use the **Paste** button in order to insert the settings in another **Standard** material inside your project. There is no need to save or load a material set.

   Great, we now can copy and paste materials in Lumion. However, we want to save this specific material so that it can be used later in another project. For this, perform the following steps:

   1. On the same panel, click on the **Save material** button.

   2. A new window appears, and you can save the material by giving it a name and saving it as a **Lumion material file**.

   3. You can try to apply another **Standard** material to a 3D model in another scene.

   4. Select the **Load material** button, and pick the file you just saved.

   5. Lumion loads the information, and all the settings are applied to the **Standard** material.

There's more...

Remember that you can use the **Reload model and re apply materials** button in case you have made some changes to the 3D model; this option will load the changes, but at the same time, it'll keep the materials applied. Lumion's website mentions that if you import a model that uses over 100 MB of texture memory, Lumion will restrict the maximum texture resolution at 2048 x 2048 pixels. However, you can bypass this limit by pressing *Alt* while you click on the **Reload model** button; this is something worth to know.

Another point is the fact that the option to copy and paste the material settings will only copy the texture information if you have loaded the textures previously. What I mean is that we can use the **Standard** material to tweak and adjust the materials that were imported along with the 3D model, but we don't necessarily need to load the textures because they are already present. However, if you want to use the **Copy** and **Paste** buttons, you need to load those textures again in order for them to be copied.

Streaming water

There are different ways in which we can add water to our project. We can create an ocean as easily as reading this sentence, and the same is true when we need to add a body of water or create a swimming pool. However, what if we want to create a fountain? Let's go even further: can we create a river? This recipe will teach you how easy is to create a streaming water effect.

Getting ready

Before you begin, it is essential that you have a surface with some inclination; otherwise, this material will not have the same effect.

How to do it...

To create a streaming water effect, perform the following steps:

1. From the left-hand side of the screen, select the **Import** menu.
2. Select the **Edit materials** button and pick a surface to add a new material.

3. Although there is a **Water** material available, you need to select the **Waterfall** material, as shown in the next screenshot:

4. The settings, by default, are good to use in almost every scene.

5. The **Bump factor** option is essential to have the effect of water flowing.

6. Adjust the **Tiling** option if the water is large in proportion to the surface.

7. Adjust the **Foam** setting according to your needs.

There's more...

It is true that we can create almost the same effect using the **Ocean** option in Lumion. However, I found that this does not always produce the best result, and in terrains with a certain inclination, the **Ocean** material will merely not meet our needs. However, in order to use this **Waterfall** material, it is essential and crucial that we have a surface with at least a small inclination; otherwise, the water will have no direction to flow.

Glowing materials

Another beautiful and eye-catching effect is when we have glowing materials in our project. From light bulbs to TV screens, we can add an extra touch to our scene by using the **Standard** material to create this glow effect. This recipe is going to teach you not only how to add this glow, but also how you can use textures to produce interesting effects.

Getting ready

In order to follow this recipe, you need at least one surface to apply the material and an image with alpha channel information.

How to do it...

To create the glow effect on a 3D model, perform the following steps:

1. On the left-hand side of the screen, select the **Import** menu. Select the **Edit materials** button and select the 3D model to add a new material.

2. Click on the **Add material** button, and after selecting a surface, apply the **Standard** material.

3. To create the glow effect, you need to increase the **Emissiveness** value.

4. To change the color of the glow effect, use the **Color** button to select a new color.

There's more...

This is a simple recipe, but the fun doesn't stop here. If you load a black and white image in the **Diffuse** slot, you can create really nice effects, as you can see in the following screenshot:

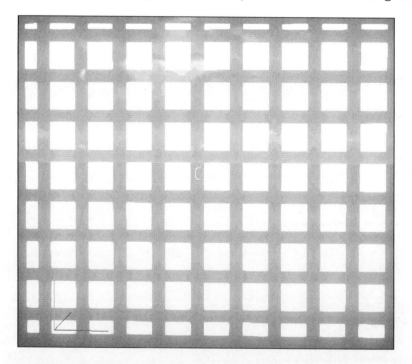

To do this, first you need an image with information in the alpha channel, and secondly, you have to adjust the **Reflection/Clip/Bright** setting to the value of **1**. When you use a texture with an alpha channel, you can clip the surface and the white area shows the surface and the black area hides or clips the surface. I use this feature in some projects when I need to fake the ceiling lights in offices, in particular, those lights that have several lamps inside.

Adding realistic grass

After adding trees, bushes, and other plants, the next thing you should add to the project is some grass. Prior to Lumion Version 4, you had to be satisfied with the terrain's texture. We can also import some grass, though, the project would become very heavy. You can also add some grass from the Lumion library and adjust that grass in the best way possible. Now, Lumion provides an option to use realistic grass, bringing that whoa factor.

Getting ready

To use this recipe, you don't need anything specific, just a terrain to see how you can add grass to your project.

How to do it...

1. From the left-hand side of the screen, select the **Landscape** menu.
2. Click on the **Grass** button, and after that, click on the **Grass on/off** button.
3. Congratulations! Now you have grass in your scene.
4. After switching on the **Grass** button, a few options will become available that will allow you to tweak the grass, as you can see in the following screenshot:

5. The **Grass Size** option controls the density of the grass and how far-out this grass will be visible.
6. The **Grass Wildness** setting is great to create an effect of a tight garden with the grass trimmed. If you increase the value, you can start adding a variety of different heights and scatter patterns to the grass.
7. Next to these settings, you can see eight squares. In order to access them, you need to click on the **Edit Type** button, the one with an arrow.
8. This action opens a new window where you can select some elements to scatter in your lawn.
9. Select an element and you will go back to the **Build** mode.
10. A small pop-up window appears above the thumbnail where you can control the **Spread**, **Size**, and **Random Size** settings.
11. With the **Spread** option, the lower the value, the more elements you will have scattered in your grass.

The first time we apply the grass, we will love this amazing feature. However, after a while, we can see that something is not quite right. The problem we face when using this grass in any project is that when we switch on the grass option, it appears in the entire landscape. This might be fine when we are working on residential projects, but if we move to a more urban space, we don't want to see grass everywhere; besides this, the grass will intersect with the 3D model at places that we don't want it to. Let's see how we can use this option in a more effective way.

To apply the grass effect on specific areas, perform the following steps:

1. From the left-hand side of the screen, select the **Import** menu.
2. Click on the **Edit materials** button and select the surface you wish to add to the grass.
3. From the **Custom** library, choose the **Landscape** material.
4. Now, when you click on the **Grass on/off** button in the **Landscape** menu, the grass appears on the surface where you applied the **Landscape** material.
5. However, this is only half of the solution because you still have the grass on the ground, and as mentioned, this grass can appear and intersect with the 3D models in places that we don't want to.
6. To solve this issue, select the **Landscape** menu.
7. Select the **Paint** menu so that you will be able to paint the terrain using the brushes.
8. The four thumbnails represent the materials used in the terrain, as you can see in the following screenshot:

9. The first thumbnail has the grass icon on it, and this shows that no matter what texture you choose, the grass is always activated.
10. Select one of the other three textures and start painting the terrain.
11. As you can see on your preceding screen, the grass will be removed from the area where you want to paint.

There's more...

This is without a doubt a fantastic feature that is available in Lumion, and the difference between using the terrain grass texture and using this realistic grass can really bring out the best in your project. Why don't you try to add the **Foliage wind** effect to the **Movie** mode and see the result? Trust me; you will really enjoy looking at the result.

I use this feature in some projects even when I don't need any grass. The reason why I do this is because in some situations, I scatter some elements that come with the grass, such as small rocks, flowers, and leaves, but I don't add grass to such projects. To be able to do this, set the **Grass size** value to **0.1** and the grass disappears; however, other elements are retained.

Improving reflections

Each material has a certain amount of reflection, and this is a setting that we can adjust in almost every material that we can find in Lumion. Taking into account that Lumion is a real-time application, it is natural that in some cases, the reflections don't meet our requirements in terms of accuracy. Lumion has an effect that we can apply to surfaces in our 3D model to improve these reflections.

Getting ready

Before you start, you need to understand that first of all, the less the number of polygons you have on the surface, the better. So, if you have a building with a huge facade, instead of using multiple surfaces, if possible, use only one surface for the entire facade. The same applies to a floor or other surface you want to add these effects to.

The second point is that you need to do the UV mapping for the surface, which will be really easy and simple if you have a surface without many polygons. This second point is not mandatory, but if you do it, you can take advantage of a **Normalmap** texture to give an extra touch.

How to do it...

To improve the reflections of a surface, perform the following steps:

1. From the left-hand side of the screen, select the **Import** menu and click on the **Edit materials** button.

2. Select the surface and add a new material.

3. At this stage, you can either choose to use a **Standard** material or another material from the Lumion library. If you going to use a material from the Lumion library, jump to step 6.

4. Apply the **Standard** material and load the textures on the **Diffuse** and **Normalmap** slots.

5. Adjust the **Scale** slider to the value **0** so that you will be able to use the UVs imported.

6. To see this effect in action, you need to increase the **Reflectivity** value to **1** or close to 1.

7. Click on the **OK** button to save the material.

8. From the right-hand side of the screen, select the **Photo** or **Movie** mode.

9. Click on the **New effect** button at the top-left corner of the screen.

10. From the **World** tab, select the **Reflection** effect to have access to the following settings, as you can see in the next screenshot:

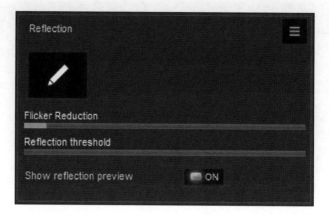

11. To add a planar reflection, click on the button with the pencil icon.

12. Click on the **Add plane** button that you can find at the bottom-left corner of the screen.

13. Lumion informs you that you need to select a **Standard** or **Glass** material to add a plane, but this will work with any material from the Lumion library.

14. Hover your mouse pointer over a surface, and a green grid appears that shows the material that will be affected by this planar reflection.

15. Click on the surface to assign the plane, and click on the **Back** button.

16. You can see a massive difference immediately, and you can use the **Show reflection preview** button to verify this.

17. The **Reflection threshold** option allows you to adjust the distance at which nearly-co-planar surfaces will be included in the reflection plane.

18. The **Normalmap** texture that you use in the **Standard** material can add some nice and interesting variations to the reflection, and you can tweak this effect by adjusting the **Bump** slider.

How it works...

With Lumion Version 4, you are limited to use 10 reflection planes in your scene. Even so, planar reflections should be used with a bit of prudence and tactic a in a scene; if possible, they should be optimized for reflections right from the start since this effect will essentially mirror your entire scene every single time you apply it. This means that with 10 reflection planes applied, your scene will also be mirrored 10 times. This will have a massive impact on the performance of your workstation, slowing down the viewport.

There's more...

This effect is ideal for mirrors, building glass facades, floors, and every element that needs accurate reflections. However, as mentioned, every time you add one reflection plane, Lumion has to mirror all the models and render the entire scene once more. So, use this option wisely and keep in mind that some materials and effects in Lumion cannot be reflected due to their limitations; these effects include **Ocean**, **Water**, **Grass**, and some other special effects.

Correcting flickering

While applying and tweaking materials, you can cross a section in your 3D model where you can easily see some flickering. Although this should be avoided, there is an inbuilt setting in every Lumion material to correct this problem. Let's see how we can use this setting.

Getting ready

To begin with this recipe, I will assume that you have the material applied to the surface, so I am skipping the steps involved for this part.

How to do it...

To remove the flickering from your 3D model, perform the following steps:

1. In the materials panel, click on the **Placing** button, and a list of options appear, as shown in the following screenshot:

2. The option you need to adjust is **Depth Offset**, but avoid making extreme adjustments.
3. Adjust the value until the flickering stops, and if necessary, press the *Shift* key to make accurate adjustments.

How it works...

This flickering happens because when two surfaces are in the same place, Lumion does not know which of the two materials should be on the front and the back. The **Depth Offset** option can correct this issue, but this situation needs to be addressed while modeling by avoiding having two surfaces in the same place.

7
Special Features

In this chapter, we will cover the following recipes:

▸ Creating fire

▸ Adding fumes and vapors

▸ Placing fountains

▸ Falling leaves

▸ Adding text

▸ Using the clip plane

▸ Controlling effects in the Movie and Photo modes

▸ Checking effects in real time

Introduction

Lumion is a marvelous application if we take into account the incredible results we can get with just a few hours of work. The lighting, the materials, the landscape, and the weather elements are essential to build a good foundation and create astonishing renders. Nevertheless, we can go the extra mile for this project by using unique effects. Special effects and features have their place for producing an eye-catching still image or a movie. They are add-ons to create a more believable environment and a world that we can recognize and feel comfortable in.

However, adding special effects to a scene should be like eating a dessert after the main meal. Using a small quantity of well-placed special effects will make all the difference between a nice image and an amazing image. However, if you overdo, the result could be an exaggerated and unpleasant render. This chapter is aimed to help you with the most common effects that we probably use in most conventional projects, and after looking at how we can use them, we are going to check how to control them and use some built-in features.

Creating fire

Fire is a special effect that is accessible in Lumion and is one of those elements that can bring an ordinary scene to life. We may have a living room that per se is excellent with all the materials and light, but when we add fire to the fireplace, it completely transforms the room into a warm, comfortable, and welcoming living room. Alternatively, consider how the same living room can be changed to introduce a romantic scene when illuminated with candles and a fireplace. This recipe is aimed to help you apply fire and control it using the **Edit properties** menu.

Getting ready

To start, a room with a fireplace may be the best choice to see this effect in action to its fullest extent. In case you don't have any 3D model available, have a look at the **Examples** tab.

How to do it...

To create fire in a project, perform the following steps:

1. Select the **Objects** menu from the left-hand side of the screen.

2. Click on the **Effects** button to access some of the special effects. It is the button with the stars icon.

3. On top of the **Place** button, click on the thumbnail called **Change object** to access the Lumion library, as you can see in the following screenshot:

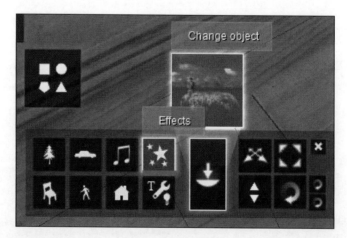

4. This action opens a new window with four tabs, and you have to click on the second tab called **Fire**.

5. From the **Fire** tab, we can choose 16 different types of fire.

6. Lumion shows an image with a woman next to each fire and this works as a reference to help you choose the fire with the correct size for the project you have.

7. Select the **fire_01** option and go back to the **Build** mode.

8. In the **Build** mode, click with the left mouse button to place the fire.

These are the fundamental steps that you will need to place a fire in any scene. However, we don't have to stop here. The following steps will give you a quick overview of how to use the **Edit properties** menu to control the settings and change the look:

1. After placing the fire, click on the **Edit properties** menu and select the fire you just placed.

2. The **Fire Properties** window opens on the right-hand side of the screen, giving you access to six settings, as you can see in the following screenshot:

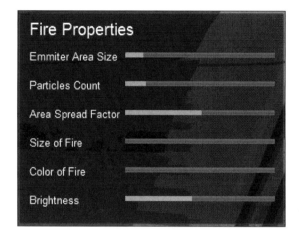

3. The **Emmiter Area Size, Area Spread Factor**, and **Size of Fire** settings control the overall size of the fire. The **Emmiter Area Size** setting is a very sensitive setting that works much better with small values.

4. Use the **Particles Count** option to change between a low, peaceful fire and a more vivid, feral fire.

There's more...

In Lumion, fire is a fantastic element because it can really bring an entire scene to life. Personally, I don't use fire in each single project, but when possible and plausible, I truly attempt to make the best use of this resource. We are not limited to fireplaces because it can make a big difference when we show, for example, a kitchen in full use with utensils, food, and the fire that plays a part in it. When we produce a 3D visualization, we also want to help out the spectator in imagining what it would be like to live there, and using this special effect will be a pleasant way to induce that feeling.

However, even after tweaking the settings, don't you feel that there is something missing? The fire effect is amazingly good, but as you can see in the **Build** mode, the fire doesn't produce any light effect on the surroundings. To get that effect, we need to use a red/orange light in order to mimic the light produced by the fire.

To use this light, you need to select the **Lights and special objects** button and then click on the **Change object** button. In the **OmniLight** tab, you can find a red light that can be used along with the fire, and trust me, once you adjust the color and the **Overbright** setting, it will make a massive difference. It is also true that there is no smoke, but we will see that in the next recipe.

Adding fumes and vapors

In addition to the solid and liquid elements in Lumion, we can find elements that we could label as non-solid. Lumion has a special section for these elements, opening with the smoke, passing all the way through dust, and then finishing with fog and water vapor. How we can place these elements in our project and a realistic application of some of them is what this recipe is going to teach you.

Getting ready

Possibly, the best way to become familiarized with these elements is by using a simple scene where we can run a smooth simulation without overcharging Lumion.

How to do it...

To add smoke to your project, perform the following steps:

1. From the left-hand side of the screen, select the **Objects** menu.
2. Click on the **Effects** button to access these special effects.
3. On top of the **Place** button, click on the thumbnail called **Change object** to access the Lumion library.
4. Once inside the **Effects Library**, start by selecting the **Smoke** tab.
5. From this tab, you can choose from 20 types of smoke; click on the first thumbnail to select the **smoke_01** option.
6. After selecting this smoke, you are directed back to the **Build** mode, and the yellow bounding box defines the area that this smoke will affect.
7. The big white arrow shows you where the smoke will be placed, and this can help you place this element accurately. Click with the left mouse button to place the smoke.

8. Select the **Edit properties** menu and select the smoke you just placed.

9. The **Smoke Properties** window opens on the right-hand side of the screen, giving you access to six settings, out of which four settings can be seen in the following screenshot:

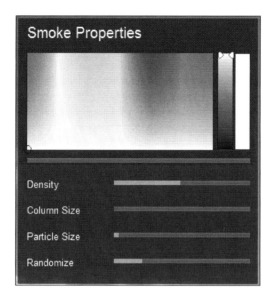

10. Adjust the **Density** slider to increase or decrease the opacity, but higher values may not produce the best results.

11. The **Particle Size** setting lets you change between the thicknesses of the smoke column.

12. Use the **Randomize** setting to adjust the way the column of fire rises. This setting helps you scatter the smoke while rising to the sky.

Next to the **Smoke** tab, we can locate the **Fog** tab. Inside this tab, we find a few additional elements to use in a scene. The fog, dust, steam, and waterdust all work in a similar way, and the reason for this is that they all use the same emitter.

If you place these four elements next to one another and check the window with the properties, they all say **Fog Properties**; the only difference will be the settings and color. So, for the next recipe, we are going to use fog. To place these elements, follow steps 1 to 8 mentioned in the previous recipe, *Adding fumes and vapors*. Let's see how we can use the **Edit properties** menu to control this with the following steps:

1. Select the **Edit properties** menu and select the fog you just placed.

2. The **Fog Properties** window opens on the right-hand side of the screen, giving you access to the following settings:

3. You can select the color using the color picker, and this is what creates the difference between the fog, dust, waterdust, and steam.

4. The **Animation Speed** setting controls the speed with which these elements will scatter across your scene.

How it works...

Although we have 20 different types of smokes in this section, in reality, they work more like a shortcut to get an effect without having to tweak the available settings. If you use the **smoke_01** option and tweak the settings, you easily get the other 19 smoke types.

There's more...

No doubt, all these effects look great, but you may wonder if they are very useful after all. The smoke is probably the one that seems to have the most practical use of something, say, a fireplace or a chimney. However, I found some practical applications of these elements, and truth be told, I don't use these effects in every single project due to the nature of the project I work with. For example, this effect works really well in a kitchen, where you can put smoke over a hot cup.

I must bring to your attention that you can control these elements (smoke and vapor) in two other ways. We can scale and rotate them, and in particular, the scale option can help us modify these elements, thereby suiting our needs. The fog can be used in a project where the house is perhaps surrounded by a forest, and this is great to reproduce mist or a cold and rainy day. The water vapor can be used to reproduce the vapor that comes out of ventilation, and if you scale it down and reduce the brightness, it can mimic the vapor from a hot tub.

Placing fountains

Fountains have their distinctive place in Lumion, and there is a tab dedicated to different categories of fountains. We can separate this tab into two parts: standard fountains and fountains produced by a waterspray emitter. This recipe is aimed to show you where to find these fountains, how to place them in the scene, and also provide you with some useful applications.

Getting ready

Possibly, the best way to become familiarized with these elements is by using a simple scene where we can run a smooth simulation without overcharging Lumion.

How to do it...

To create a fountain in your scene, perform the following steps:

1. From the left-hand side of the screen, select the **Objects** menu.
2. Click on the **Effects** button.
3. Select the thumbnail called **Change object** to access the Lumion library.
4. The first tab is the one that contains all the fountains that are available.
5. Select one of the first 19 fountains and place it in your scene.
6. With this kind of fountain, you can only move, rotate, and scale. If you scale the fountain, keep in mind that this will change the speed of the water.
7. Click on the **Edit properties** menu and select the fountain.
8. The only settings available to change are the **X**, **Y**, and **Z** coordinates.
9. Go back to the **Effects** Library.
10. After the **Fountain019** option, you will find another fountain called **fountainround_01**. Select it and place it in your project.

11. If you check the properties of this fountain, the following are the settings that are available:

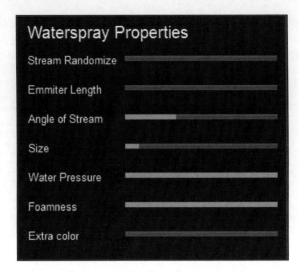

12. The same principle we saw previously is applied with this element, that is, if you adjust the settings, you can reproduce all the other fountains available using one fountain.

13. Adjust the **Emmiter Length** setting to change between a fountain with a round shape and a straight line.

14. The **Angle of Stream** and the **Water Pressure** settings have almost the same effect. You can keep the **Water Pressure** setting with the value of **1** and use the **Angle of Stream** setting to adjust the pressure.

15. Use the **Stream Randomize** setting to create a far more interesting fountain. You can get the best results with values above **0.2**.

There's more...

Fountains may not be the number one element to use in a scene because, generally, not every project requires a fountain. Yet, I find this special element to be very useful when creating swimming pools. To create a swimming pool, a little bit more credible, we can use these fountains; we can also control the settings to put them under the water line and on top of the grids to mimic water that is pumped inside the pool.

Another application is using a fountain to replicate the sprinkles that you can find in a garden irrigation. Reducing the **Water Pressure** value and increasing the **Stream Randomize** value creates a really nice effect.

Falling leaves

Falling leaves are an enjoyable extra touch that can improve our still image or movie. Nevertheless, like the preceding special effects, this one needs to be used in the correct amount. Too much can ruin the scene, making the viewer focus more on leaves passing through the screen than actually focus on the 3D model.

Getting ready

For this recipe, you can just use a standard terrain to play with this effect. If you want to add a tree to your project, this effect can become more believable.

How to do it...

To make leaves fall in your scene, perform the following steps:

1. From the left-hand side of the screen, select the **Objects** menu.
2. Click on the **Effects** button to access these special effects.
3. Use the **Change object** thumbnail to access the Lumion library.
4. Once inside the **Effects Library**, click on the last tab called **Leaves**.
5. Select the first object called **leaves_01** and place it in your project.
6. Click on the **Edit properties** menu and select the leaves to gain access to the **Falling leaves Properties** settings, as shown in the following screenshot:

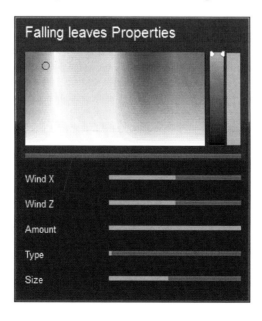

7. The **Amount** setting controls the number of leaves generated, but remember that the leaves are generated from the middle of the bounding box.

8. If you want to have more leaves falling down, use the **Change height** button to bring the leaves up. The leaves are not constrained by the bounding box.

9. By default, the **Wind X** and **Wind Z** settings have the value of **0**, and this is what makes the leaves fall on the ground.

10. Adjust the **Wind X** and **Wind Z** settings to move the leaves along one or both the axes.

11. The **Foliage wind** effect doesn't affect the leaves, so use the **Wind X** and **Wind Z** settings to control the flow and direction of the falling leaves.

How it works...

In the **Leaves** tab, we find three objects, but there is no special difference between them. We could say they are based on the **leaves_01** option but with different settings.

There's more...

This special effect is good when we have some trees in the project, but it is specially useful to produce a nice autumn scene. In order to do that, you need to change the tree properties, in particular, the **Green selection hue** setting, to get the leaves with the yellow color.

Do you know what great effect you can get with these falling leaves? Fireflies! This may somehow sound strange, but if you reduce the **Size** and **Amount** setting of the leaves, you need to crank up the **Overbright** setting to a really high value. Use this for a night scene, and the result will be fantastic.

Adding text

We can add text to a movie or a still image using the **Titles** effect, but in some circumstances, we need a text element with some more flexibility. Sometimes, when working on a presentation of a project, we are required to show some additional information; this can be easily achieved using this fantastic feature available in Lumion. Let's see how we can add text to our project in the **Build** mode.

Getting ready

Nothing special is really needed; a flat terrain will work so that you can see and test this functionality.

How to do it...

To add text to your scene, perform the following steps:

1. From the **Build** mode, select the **Objects** menu.
2. Click on the **Lights and special objects** option and open the library of this option.
3. Inside the **Lights and Utilities Library**, click on the **Utilities** tab.
4. Select the **text simple** object.
5. Place this object and open the properties panel using the **Edit properties** button.
6. The **Text Properties** window is really complete with the options, as shown in the following screenshot:

7. The **Fade Range** setting controls the yellow circle and the **Visible Range** setting controls the blue circle that you can see on the ground.
8. The **Visible Range** setting defines when you can start seeing the text, but the **Fade Range** setting helps in creating a smooth transition between the text that appears and disappears from the view.

9. The **Height** setting moves the text up and at the same time creates a sort of arrow that points to the point where it was placed.

10. By default, the text will always face the camera no matter what the angle is, but with the **Style** orientation set to **3**, you can create something similar to a static sign.

Using the clip plane

A clip plane is an object that can be added to a scene and later used in the **Movie** mode, and it can be animated to produce a kind of reveling effect. Initially, it may seem a little bit confusing, but after reading this recipe, you will understand how to apply it to your scene and animate this plane.

Getting ready

To begin this recipe, add some 3D models to your scene in order to see how this effect works.

How to do it...

To add and use the clip plane, you need to perform the following steps:

1. From the left-hand side of the screen, select the **Objects** menu and click on the **Lights and special objects** button.

2. Open **Lights And Utilities Library** and click on the **Utilities** tab.

3. Place the clip plane in the scene and almost everything will disappear.

4. Click on the **Change height** button and start to bring the place upward.

5. As you can perceive, while moving the clip plane upward, you can start seeing the 3D models in your terrain again.

6. Everything below the clip plane is shown, and everything above the clip plane is hidden.

This clip plane becomes useful only when you move to the **Movie** mode. You may consider creating a layer to control and hide this clip plane while working in the **Build** mode; this can be done with the following steps:

1. Go to the **Movie** mode.

2. Create a small clip if necessary in order to apply the next effect that will control this clip plane.

3. Click on the **New effect** button and open the **Objects** tab.

4. You can create a simple animation to control the clip plane in a more effective way by using the **Move** effect.

5. Select the **Move** effect and move this module to the **Movie** mode interface, as you can see in the following screenshot:

6. Click on the **Move** button to access the tools to animate the clip plane by defining the start and end position.

There's more...

The clip plane is an interesting feature that can be used to show the 3D models to the viewer gradually, creating that animation style where you can show buildings that rise from the ground and some elements of the construction to the viewer. However, this clip plane option is limited because it will not clip plants and we cannot use it just for a specific area. This doesn't mean that it is impossible to create complex animations, but it will involve exterior tools to create such a composition.

One workaround is inverting the typical animation of the 3D models in which they raise from the ground by placing the clip plane at a certain height and then making the 3D models "fall" from above.

See also

▶ To learn how to create a clip, check the *Creating a camera path* recipe in *Chapter 10, Bringing Your World to Life*

Controlling effects in the Movie and Photo modes

It is time to move from special effects, such as fire, smoke, and water that we can add to the scene and move towards effects that we can apply in both the **Movie** and **Photo** modes. We are not going to cover the different effects available in both these modes. Instead, the goal of this recipe is to give you an overview of how general effects work, how you can stack them in either the **Movie** or **Photo** mode, and how you can control them.

Getting ready

For this tutorial, you will need to have some clips in the **Movie** mode so that you will be able to test this recipe properly.

How to do it...

Let's start by adding some effects; this can be done by performing the following steps:

1. From the right-hand side of the screen, select the **Photo** mode.

2. Click on the **New effect** button.

3. Add some effects to your image. It doesn't need to be anything in particular because we are going to focus on another feature, but you can add the **Sun study**, **Shadow**, and **Global Illumination** effects.

4. If you have applied the previous effects, a few things will change in the interface.

5. Next to the **Build with effects** button, you have a new menu to navigate between effects, as you can see in the following screenshot:

6. Next to the **New effect** button is the **Copy** button to copy all the effects.

7. Click on the **Copy** button and go back to the **Movie** mode to see how it works.

8. Select a clip and click on the **Paste** button.

9. As you can see, you can copy effects from the **Photo** mode to the **Movie** mode.

10. Also, each effect you add will have a button on the top-right corner of the screen that will give you access to the following options:

11. The **Remove** and **Hide** options are self-explanatory, but we want to turn our attention to the **Move...** option.

12. Select the **Move...** option and another two options will appear: the **Up** and **Down** buttons. These two buttons allow you to move the selected effect between other effects.

How it works...

Although this feature to move the effect up and down in the stack of effects doesn't look too important, it can actually affect your scene. A good illustration of this is when you add the **Snow** effect rather than the **Rain** effect; this last action will cancel the **Snow** effect. Of course, this doesn't happen with all the effects, but it is good to keep in mind that some effects can cancel the previous ones. So, this option of moving the effect can help verify whether the effect is in the correct stack position.

Checking effects in real time

It is logical that all the effects available in Lumion are applied using either the **Movie** or **Photo** mode. The reason for this is that if all those effects were applied to the **Build** mode, they would have a massive impact on the performance of the viewport, slowing down our workflow. However, Lumion likes to provide you with the freedom needed to produce the best result possible, and in some situations, it could be useful to check the effects in the **Build** mode. Let's see how we can do that.

Getting ready

To use this recipe, you need some effects applied to your image or movie.

How to do it...

To check the effects in the **Build** mode, perform the following steps:

1. In the **Movie** or **Photo** mode, apply some effects to your project.

2. Click on the **Build with effects** button, as shown in the following screenshot:

3. When you click on this button, you go back to the **Build** mode, but in this instance, all the effects will be applied.

4. Move your mouse to the left-hand side of the screen; notice that you can still access the **Landscape**, **Import**, and **Objects** menus.

5. The beauty of this feature is that it provides the opportunity to add or remove the 3D models, change materials and the landscape, and then see the effects in action.

6. Click on the **Back** button to return to either the **Movie** or **Photo** mode. There is another feature that we will explore in this recipe and that is using the **Theater** button.

7. Return to the recipe and go to the **Movie** mode.

8. At the bottom-right corner of the screen, there is a small button with the play icon called **Theater**, as you can see in the following screenshot:

9. Click on this button, and you will be able to access a sort of lite version of the **Build** mode.

10. You can use the arrows or *WASD* keys to move the effect and press the left mouse button to look around.

11. Click on the **Back** button to return to the **Movie** mode.

There's more...

The **Theater** mode, for some reason, only works with all the effects if you are using them in the **Movie** mode. Also, if you click on the **Play** button and then click on the **Theater** mode button, the camera will follow the animation you have assigned to it.

The **Theater** mode is very useful when we don't have time to render a movie or we want to go with the client and explore and verify the 3D models and materials together. It is really useful when you are giving presentations to a group of people and you need the space to go back and forth in your presentation.

8
Getting Realism with Camera Effects

In this chapter, we will cover the following recipes:

- ▶ Using the Bloom effect
- ▶ Adding lens' errors
- ▶ Correcting the colors
- ▶ Separating objects with DOF
- ▶ Simulating the Lens flare effects
- ▶ Using God rays
- ▶ Adding noise
- ▶ Isolating colors with Lumion
- ▶ Using the Vignette effect
- ▶ Sharpening your image

Introduction

Lumion is not an application that is intended to produce hyper-realistic images or videos. Nevertheless, in Lumion, we can find some camera effects that assist in producing a more credible still image or movie, and this chapter will be more technical as we are going to look at some vital points in photography.

The artifacts that a photographer generally wants to remove, such as chromatic aberration, vignette, and noise, are the elements we want to add to our image or video. These undesirable aspects for a photographer are what we need to add in order to make it more realistic, without overdoing it. The golden rule is that if we start to see the effect clearly, it means that it is time to stop applying it. First, we need to fully understand what an effect is before we can correctly apply it. This is because in some situations, the required effect doesn't get applied and the image or video looks artificial. So, in all the recipes in this chapter, we will explore what an effect is and how we can apply it to our project. You may find it strange to not see screenshots of the effects applied to the scene, but the reason why we are not showing any of them is because the effects need to be subtle and you can hardly see any difference in the screenshots. The best way to get familiarized with the effects mentioned is by playing with them in the following recipes.

Using the Bloom effect

Bloom is the halo effect caused principally by bright lights in the scene. In real world, the camera lenses we use can never focus perfectly, but this is not a problem under normal conditions. However, when there is an intensely bright light in the scene, these imperfections are perceptible and visible, and as a consequence, in the photo that we would shoot, the bright light will appear to bleed beyond its usual borders.

Getting ready

To fully understand the usage of this effect, it will be good if you have an interior with a daylight scene or a scene with some artificial lights.

How to do it...

To add the **Bloom** effect to an image or a video, perform the following steps:

1. From the right-hand side of the screen, select either the **Photo** or **Movie** mode.
2. In case you select the **Movie** mode, make sure that you click on a clip to apply the effect.
3. Click on the **New effect** button to access the library with the effects.
4. From the **Style** tab, select the **Bloom** effect.
5. The **Bloom** effect is applied to your scene and you can immediately see how it transforms your project drastically.
6. Use the **Bloom** module to adjust this effect to something more pleasant and not so strong.

There's more...

The **Bloom** effect that we just added to the project is a natural effect and depends on the lens and the intensity of the light. This happens in real life when, for example, we are filming or shooting inside a building during the daytime with a window in the frame, and because the exposure of the camera is set for interior light, the daylight will bleed slightly out of the window frame. With Lumion, this is a little bit difficult to achieve because the **Bloom** effect will increase the brightness of every highlight in your project; however, it can still be used to improve the bloom effect in bright light by removing some of the CG look.

Adding lens' errors

Purple fringing, distortion, and blurred edges are a combination of errors called chromatic aberration. A simple explanation is that chromatic aberration happens when there is a failure on the part of lens to focus or bring all the wavelengths of colors to the same focal plane. As light travels through this lens, the different colors travel at different speeds and go to different places on the camera's sensor. With 3D cameras, this doesn't happen, but we can add chromatic aberration to our image or video, giving an extra touch of realism.

Getting ready

You can see this effect in a better way in an exterior scene, but if you just want to observe this effect in action, use the **Villa** scene found in the **Examples** tab.

How to do it...

To add chromatic aberration, you need to perform the following steps:

1. Select the **Movie** or **Photo** mode.
2. Click on the **New effect** button and open the **Artistic** tab.
3. Add the **Chromatic Aberrations** effect and the following settings will become available:

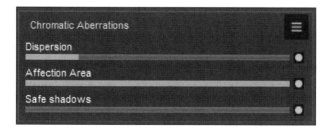

4.   Look at your image again, and if necessary, use the **Hide** function in the **Chromatic Aberrations** effect to verify the difference before and after this effect is applied.

5.   The settings used by default provide a good start, and in most projects, you should aim to reduce the effect and not increase it.

6.   The **Dispersion** setting controls the amount of chromatic aberration in an image or video.

7.   The chromatic aberration starts from the sides of your frame and goes towards the center, and you can tweak that using the **Affection Area** slider.

8.   Adjust the **Safe shadows** setting to remove the chromatic aberration from the dark and shaded areas, thereby preserving the details.

There's more...

Be cautious with this effect; when you start noticing the chromatic aberration, it means that it is time to step back a little bit and stop there. Too much of this effect will ruin your scene, and in some circumstances, it will make no sense at all to use it; this is why it is very important to understand what chromatic aberration is and why it happens. With this knowledge, we can evaluate the project we are working on and whether this effect will bring something as a final output.

Black and white photos or movies are also affected by chromatic aberration, but in this situation, chromatic aberration will blur the image.

Correcting the color

The expression "color correction" has a fair number of different meanings. However, generally speaking, we can say that it is a means to repair problems with the color, and we do that by changing the color of a pixel to another color or by tweaking other settings. In Lumion, this means that we can use color correction to either achieve a certain look or to enhance the overall aspect and mood of an image or a movie. Let's see how we can use this effect in Lumion and look at a few tips to help us not only to correct the color, but also perform some color grading.

Getting ready

In case you want to test this effect and play with it before using it in your scene, open the **Villa** scene found in the **Examples** tab. It will be good if you have the **Movie** or **Photo** mode already open.

How to do it...

To color correct your image or video, perform the following steps:

1. Click on the **New effect** button and open the **Style** tab.

2. In the **Style** tab, select the **Color correction** effect and the following settings will be inserted into your scene:

3. There are some self-explanatory settings, such as **Brightness**, **Contrast**, and **Enhance contrast**, but we are going to explain what the additional settings can bring to your scene in a better way.

4. The **Gamma** slider will adjust the midtones, and this should not be confused with the **Brightness** setting because the **Gamma** setting doesn't increase the highlights. So, they work in different areas although initially it doesn't look like that.

5. With the **Saturation** setting, you can apply contrast; however, instead of increasing the separation between shadows and highlights, it will increase the separation between colors.

6. The **Red Shift** and **Blue Shift** settings should be used together because when you increase one setting, the other needs to be decreased.

7. To add a warmer feeling to your scene, increase the **Ref Shift** value and decrease the **Blue Shift** value; do the reverse to apply a colder look.

There's more...

There is a limit of how much can be fixed or done using the color correction effect, and to be honest, we should use this effect more to add or modify a color tint instead of trying to change something that is green to blue. Habitually, color correction is used to make the scene more vivid or improve some elements, such as bringing out a little bit more of the color of the sky or water.

Another thing we could try to do with this effect is color grading. Color grading is giving the final look and feel to your image or video. A technique to do some color grading is turning down the **Saturation** and **Contrast** settings by just a small amount to preserve the details on the shadows and highlights; then you tweak the **Red Shift** and **Blue Shift** settings to achieve an interesting effect, but at the same time, provide a subtle look. If you need to perform a more specific color grading, such as splitting colors and perform some hue shifts, you will probably need an external application, for example, Premiere or After Effects.

Separating objects with DOF

Depth of field (**DOF**) refers to the range of distance in front and behind an element that appears acceptably sharp. To give an example, imagine that we want to focus on a tree but not on other elements of the environment, such as the house behind, the grass on the ground, the swimming pool, and other elements. In real world, with the correct combination of lens and aperture, it is possible to focus only on the tree and all the other elements will be out of focus. Lumion has a fantastic DOF effect very close to a real camera.

Getting ready

To test this recipe, it is essential that you have some objects in your project, and what would be especially useful is to ensure that the 3D models have different distances between them. Also, go to the **Movie** or **Photo** mode in order to apply this effect.

How to do it...

To add DOF to your project, perform the following steps:

1. Click on the **New effect** button and open the **Camera** tab.
2. Select the **Depth of Field** effect, and if you have some experience with photography, you will recognize some of the settings available, as shown in the next screenshot:

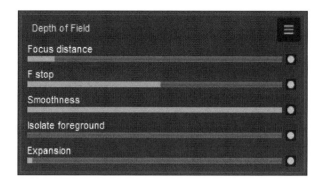

3. First, keep in mind that the **Focal length (mm)** value that you use to create a clip or a photo doesn't come into the equation.

4. The **Focus distance** should be the first setting adjusted to define where you want your camera to focus.

5. Then, tweak the **F stop** setting to remove some of the blur areas and define the gradual transition between the sharp and blurred areas.

6. **Isolate foreground** is a setting that controls the layers of DOF in front of the camera. However, these settings will not always produce the best result, in particular, with trees.

7. When zooming too close to an object, you may need to adjust the **Expansion** setting in order to get a sharp look of the 3D model.

8. Don't forget to press the *Shift* key while adjusting these settings in small increments.

There's more...

DOF has a deep impact on the artistic and technical quality of a picture, and it will provide a singular touch to the movie or photo you are going to create. DOF is also useful when you want to direct the viewer to a specific point in a picture, and because this will blur the background and the foreground details, all the distractions will melt away. Nevertheless, we need to adjust the DOF settings when producing a movie, and for that, we need to keyframe the settings to achieve a natural and beautiful outcome. This will take some time and testing, but hurry is the enemy of perfection.

Simulating the Lens flare effects

Lens flare is an artifact (usually in the shape of a lens iris) and a common problem for photographers that is caused when direct light hits the front of the lens, and in photography, this light is called **non-image forming light**. Although this is often an undesired artifact, some types of lens flares are used to enhance the artistic meaning of a photo. By default, Lumion applies this lens flare in your scene in a very subtle way, but let's see how we can control it using the **Lens flare** effect.

Getting ready

To use this recipe, you can have a simple scene in order to understand this effect, and it will be great if the sun is in the frame with Lumion's camera. Also, go to the **Movie** or **Photo** mode in order to apply this effect.

How to do it...

To add the **Lens flare** effect to your scene, perform the following steps:

1. Insert a new effect by clicking on the **New effect** button.
2. Select the **Camera** tab and then select the **Lens flare** effect to access the following settings:

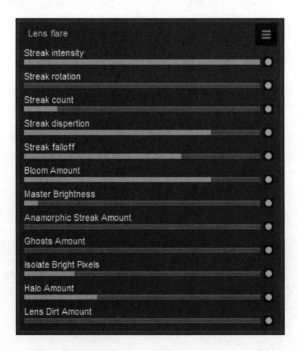

3. The seven initial settings control the overall aspect of the light's source that causes the lens flare.

4. The **Anamorphic Streak Amount** setting is a lens flare caused by the use of anamorphic lenses, which are often used during the production of films, and this will make more sense if you use it in a movie.

5. To manage the amount of artifacts in your scene, tweak the **Ghosts Amount** and **Isolate Bright Pixels** settings to increase or decrease the brightness of these artifacts.

6. One of the best settings of these effects is the **Lens Dirt Amount** setting that will add dirt particles to the lens of the camera, but remember the golden rule.

There's more...

Although this is a great effect that we can add to our image or movie, we need to use it in a subtle way. The point is not to show that we can add a lens flare, but to try and mimic the real world we live in instead. For this reason, we should take some time to search for an example where a lens flare was used in an artistic way to enhance the photograph. When using these effects, always work with references and not from memory.

Using God rays

There is a compilation of atmospheric optics that are part of our daily life, although sometimes we don't realize this. Some of them are the rainbow, sunset colors, aurora, crepuscular rays, and solar rays. In computer graphics, these solar rays are also called God rays, and these are the rays of sunlight that stream through the gaps in the clouds and appear to radiate from a point in the sky where the sun is located. God rays can really add some impact to our project, and Lumion has a fantastic effect to mimic these rays. Let's see how we can use it.

Getting ready

Before you use this effect, it is imperative to have clouds in the sky within the scene because this is the best way to perceive this effect in real life, and the same happens in Lumion.

How to do it...

To add solar or God rays to your scene, perform the following steps:

1. Go to the **Movie** or **Photo** mode and make sure you have some clouds in the sky.

2. Click on the **New effect** button to open the effects library.

3. From the **Artistic** tab, select the **God rays** effect.

4.   Once more, there are two essential elements to fully use the **God rays** effect, and the following screenshot shows you both of these:

5.   The sun is the first element that is required, and you will get better results if the sun is in the frame of your camera; however, this is not crucial. The image on the right-hand side of the screenshot though has the sun and the **God rays** effect applied and still we cannot see any rays.

6.   The second element that plays a key role as you can see on the left-hand side of the preceding screenshot is clouds.

7.   Use the **VolumeClouds** effect to achieve a better result for your final image or movie.

8.   In addition, adjust the **Decay** slider to control the brightness of these rays.

Adding noise

Noise or digital noise are terms used to describe the flecks, random points, or grain that will visually distort the photograph when shooting in low light. Noise, in general, occurs when the illumination is low and the digital sensor attempts to record even tiny amounts of light; as a result, noise will get introduced in the photograph. Let's see how we can do that using the **Noise** effect in Lumion.

Getting ready

To prepare for this recipe, go to the **Movie** or **Photo** mode depending on the final output you desire.

How to do it...

To add some noise to your project, perform the following steps:

1. On the top-left corner of the screen, click on the **New effect** button.
2. With the effects library open, go to the **Style** tab.
3. Select the **Noise** effect, and you will perceive that the viewport has changed; now it has a type of noise that is added, known as white noise.
4. The settings available to control the noise in your project are shown in the following screenshot:

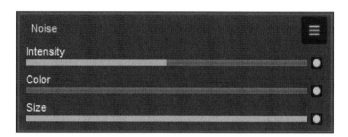

5. You can create colored noise using the **Color** setting, but this will also make your noise stronger and perceptible.
6. The **Intensity** slider controls the strength of the white noise, and it doesn't seem to have a huge effect when you are using colored noise.
7. The **Size** setting will work in an inverse way, and this means that the lower the value, the bigger the size of the noise.

There's more...

In a real camera, the **Noise** effect will be introduced if we use slow shutter speeds or a very high sensitivity mode. Although this is an artifact, we can add a very small amount of noise to our video or image to produce a more believable result. However, again, as mentioned in some recipes before, the secret for a believable image or video is the use of these effects in a balanced and moderate way. We can add noise to the image or video, but it really needs to be something very, and I repeat, very subtle so that the viewer will focus their attention on what we want to show and not on the noise.

How much noise is too much noise is difficult to define in some projects. However, more noise might be suitable for some night time scenes, but for an interior scene, where detail and color fidelity are essential, the same amount of noise would seem to be out of place.

Isolating colors with Lumion

A technique used in some films such as Schindler's List and Sin City is called selective color, where the photo or movie is converted to black and white with some elements that are left in color. This is a post-production technique that is usually achieved by using layers and masks, but Lumion provides a fantastic effect that will help us produce a similar effect effortlessly. This means that we don't need an external application to produce the same effect. Let's see how we can use it along with some practical applications.

Getting ready

To fully understand this effect, it will be great if you have a variety of 3D models in your scene. If you want, another good way is to pick the **Materials** scene from the **Examples** tab.

How to do it...

To isolate colors using the **Selective saturation** effect, perform the following steps:

1. From the right-hand side of the screen, select the **Movie** or **Photo** mode.
2. Open the effects library using the **New effect** button.
3. From the **Style** tab, select the **Selective saturation** effect.
4. This gives you access to five sliders to adjust your image, as shown in the following screenshot:

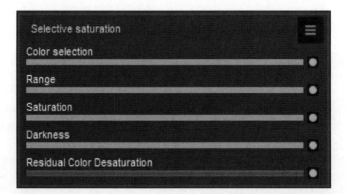

5. When you apply this effect, the colors will pop up automatically, and this is because the **Saturation** value is already set to **1**.
6. To start isolating the colors, you need to crank up the **Residual Color Desaturation** setting to a value that is close to **1**.

7. Use the **Color selection** setting to start selecting the colors. A value of **0.3** will isolate the green color, a value close to **0.5** will isolate the blue color, and a value of **0.9** will isolate the orange/brown color.

8. The **Range** slider is essential in order to see some color, and this setting can be used to isolate the color in a better way. In some situations, you may be presented with green and some blue, but if you adjust the **Range** setting, you can remove that blue color from the scene.

There's more...

Selective saturation can be a powerful technique for getting more realistic images and to tweak your final output. It is true that it can be used to isolate specific colors, and this can be useful to draw the viewer's attention to something we want to show. This is particularly useful when working on a landscape project when we need to show green spaces, plants, bushes, and the trees used.

Using this effect, we could actually change the mood of an entire project by tinting an image or movie, thereby giving it a warmer or cooler look. Another way in which we can use this effect is when we feel the need to improve the color of some elements in our project that can be a little bit dull.

Using the Vignette effect

Vignette is a French word to describe many things, but in photography, it is used to describe an unintended and undesired effect caused by the camera settings, where the corners of an image are darker when compared to the centre. Vignette is an effect that occurs naturally, and it can be rather strong or hardly noticeable; this is related to the lens used. Lumion has the same effect that can be used in our projects. Let's see how we can use it, and at the same time, why we can use this effect.

Getting ready

To use this recipe, you need to open the **Movie** mode and select a clip to add the effect to a movie or open the **Photo** mode if you want to add this effect to an image.

How to do it...

1. In the **Movie** or **Photo** mode, add a new effect using the **New effect** button.
2. Open the **Artistic** tab and select the **Vignette** effect.

3. This is a very simple effect with only two settings, as shown in the following screenshot:

4. The **Vignette Amount** setting controls the distance between the center of the image and the edges, and the **Vignette Softness** setting adjusts how strong this effect will be.

There's more...

This effect can also be added in post-processing in order to pull the viewer's attention away from the distractions in the corner towards the centre of the image. Once more, when we use this effect, it really depends on the nature of the project we are working on. When the camera is focused on a particular 3D model, **Vignette** can be used to turn this object into the centre of attention, but when doing an exterior scene, maybe, we could use a more discrete **Vignette** effect.

Sharpening your image

Sharpness is the quality of details captured in a photograph, and two factors are essential to perceive the sharpness of an image. We need a resolution and acutance. Acutance is the distinction of borders of an image, so when we use acutance, this will create an image or movie with sharp transitions between edges, increasing the detail. This means that we can give a much clearer look to an image or movie by using this effect. In Lumion, we have the **Sharpness** effect that can help us with this task.

Getting ready

To apply and perceive the effects of this effect, you need to have a variety of 3D models in your project.

How to do it...

1. On the right-hand side of the screen, click on the **Movie** or **Photo** button depending on the final output you need.
2. The **Sharpness** effect can be found in the **Style** tab.

3.   This effect is the most simplest effect that you can find in Lumion, as shown in the
     following screenshot:

4.   You have one single setting, **Intensity**, to control this effect.

5.   The value, by default, might be too strong, so you need to adjust this effect taking into
     account not only the type of project you are working on, but also the amount of detail
     present in your scene.

There's more...

This effect can be used to balance the amount of blur and DOF we may have. However,
we need to be cautious with scenes that are bursting with 3D models because if we use
too much sharpness, it can become harsh on the viewer's eyes.

9
Non-photorealistic Effects

In this chapter, we will cover the following recipes:

- ▶ Adding a Manga effect
- ▶ Using toon shading
- ▶ Painting your image
- ▶ Drawing with a pencil
- ▶ Painting with Watercolor
- ▶ Creating stills
- ▶ Using special formats
- ▶ Creating and combining different NPR effects

Introduction

Non-photorealistic render (**NPR**) is the use of artistic illustration techniques to translate a 3D environment into an image or video that does not seem to be realistic. Some NPR techniques involve the use of cross-hatching, outlines, cell shading, stippling, and impressionism, and the purpose of these techniques is to create visualizations with a style that is not constrained by the precision, fidelity, and perfection of the real world.

Lumion provides a combination of effects that can really imitate some of these techniques, but there is no such thing as automatic art. Making art is a creative, intelligent, and thoughtful process. This implies the truth that to produce an artistic and eye-catching visualization that communicates with the viewer, we need to do more than just add a nice effect. We need to use Lumion's tools to achieve our goal and not let these tools dictate what we can do. This chapter is aimed to present to you some of Lumion's artistic effects, explain what they are, and how to apply them.

Some of the recipes will probably be simple, but you need to look at the big picture and after understanding how these effects work, see how you can use them to achieve your goal.

Adding a Manga effect

One of the effects we will start exploring is the **Manga** effect. Manga refers to a style of cartoons that originated in Japan. This style of drawings is done using a pen or black and white ink and the main attribute is the use of clean lines. This recipe will help you see some possible settings' combinations to produce different results that can later be used in conjunction with other effects.

Getting ready

To use this recipe, you may want to remove some effects such as DOF that will cause weird artifacts when you apply the **Manga** effect.

How to do it...

To apply this **Manga** effect and give a cartoon effect to your scene, perform the following steps:

1. Go to the **Movie** or **Photo** mode and add a new effect. For this, you need to click on the **New effect** button, which you can find at the top-left corner of the screen.

2. From the **Artistic** tab, select the **Manga** effect.

3. On the viewport, you can see that with this effect you obtain a more cartoonish scene with enjoyable colors. You can use the **Tonecount** setting to control the amount of detail and color in the image.

4. A cool feature is the **Pattern** setting that adds a stippling texture to the image and on some occasions, removes the blotchiness you may have.

5. To achieve an outline look and remove any color, adjust the **Outline vs fill** slider to the highest value until you get a result similar to the following screenshot:

6. The **Manga** effect has a special feature. This effect can blend with the original scene, as you can see in the previous screenshot. The books still have some details of the texture used and if you look closely, you can see some texture information being used to add more detail to the wood shelf, the floor, and the wall behind.

There's more...

After working with this effect, we become aware that there is no option to have full color and at the same time have the outlines that were shown in the previous screenshot. One way to bypass this limitation is by exporting two images: one with full color without outlines and the other with only the outlines, and then combining them using an external application, such as Gimp or Photoshop. The image with the color information is the base and the image with the outlines goes on top, but you need to apply multiply effects in order to see the colors and the black lines.

Why should we do this? It really depends on what type of visualization we are looking at, but in some projects, in particular those with loads of details, this extra layer of outline will provide more depth to the image and will ensure that the viewer doesn't get confused with so much color information.

There is also FotoSketcher, a 100 percent free program for Windows, which converts your digital photos into art automatically, and in just a few mouse clicks saves the effort of exporting two images and combining them together.

Using toon shading

In some projects, it may be required that we create a quick conceptual illustration of an architectural design. These easy illustrations are an economical way to communicate a variety of construction options to the client and sometimes, it can be decisive for the final visualization. The lighting in Lumion may not always be sufficient to outline the 3D models' details and the shadows may generate ambiguous surface details and profiles. With the **Cartoon** effect, we can create these conceptual illustrations not only as colored sketches, but also as black and white illustrations.

Getting ready

As mentioned in the previous recipe, you may want to remove some effects that will cause strange artifacts when you apply them.

How to do it...

To create a conceptual visualization quickly, perform the following steps:

1. Click on the **Movie** or **Photo** mode depending on your desired final output.

2. Find the **Cartoon** effect in the **Artistic** tab.

3. The result acquired with this effect is different from the **Manga** effect because the **Cartoon** effect doesn't merge perfectly with the scene and with experience, you will find that some textures may not produce the best look and they need to be replaced with materials with full color.

4. Keep in mind that there is always a small difference between what you see in the viewport and the outcome when you export and save the image or movie.

5. Achieving a cartoon look will depend on your project and the materials used, but the following combination should give you a good start:

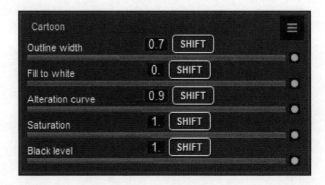

6. To produce a black and white illustration, you need to adjust the **Fill to white** setting to a value of **2**.

7. With the **Fill to white** slider set to the highest value, set the **Outline width** setting to **0** and gradually increase the value to **2**. As you will see, this will draw the outline of the 3D models present in the scene. A value higher than **1** will increase the thickness of the line, but will also pick up the detail in the interior of the 3D model.

8. The **Alteration curve** setting is used to increase or remove the brightness of the scene and it can be combined with the **Fill to white** setting to remove any gray areas.

9. By default, the **Black level** value is set to **0**, but this may remove the contrast from your scene and you may find that a value of **1** usually helps to achieve a more pleasing look.

There's more...

The **Cartoon** effect along with the **Manga** effect can produce some colored sketches that as we mentioned in the beginning of this recipe could have multiple applications. One of these applications produces technical illustrations. A technical illustration can make good use of the drawing lines generated by these two effects, and this illustration style is one of the most frequent and effective styles because it can express information in a concise and conceptual manner.

Another option is combining the results we get from the **Cartoon** and **Manga** effects. The **Cartoon** effect produces realistic and precise outlines, but the **Manga** effect can bring the extra detail from textures and bump maps.

Painting your image

Using some painting techniques to create a conceptual illustration is another possibility. Impressionist painting characteristics include fairly small and slim but nevertheless visible brush strokes, and the stress is on the overall visual effects instead of details. Lumion has an incredible effect that reproduces some of these characteristics and it can be used to produce a visualization focusing on shape and color. Let's see how we can use the **Painting** effect.

Getting ready

Before starting, it is important to remember that applying this effect over other effects, such as **Manga** or **Cartoon**, will significantly change the outcome you get from the **Painting** effect. Also, you may want to search some impressionist paintings to see the variety of styles and how you can reproduce them with this effect.

How to do it...

To give an impressionist look to your project, perform the following steps:

1. With the **Movie** or **Photo** mode open, add a new effect using the **New effect** button.

2. Navigate to the **Artistic** tab and select the **Painting** effect to add the following settings to your interface:

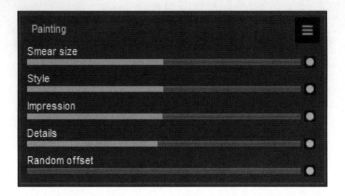

3. You will immediately see the beautiful result of this effect in your scene, particularly when you have used materials with texture information, such as wood, tiles, and bricks.

4. You can achieve a nice impressionist look with the default values, but you can tweak this look using the **Impression** slider. There are no correct values for this effect. It is just a question of taste and artistic perception.

5. The **Smear size** setting controls the paint strokes and it can be used to improve the 3D model's edges producing a more distinct look.

6. The lower value of the **Style** setting will produce a more loose painting with noticeable strokes of paint and if you increase the value, the areas in your image will be more defined.

7. The **Details** slider is self-explanatory, but the **Random offset** setting can be used when you are preparing different images to give a unique look to each one.

There's more...

You may find it worth exploring a combination of the **Cartoon** and **Painting** effects when creating this artistic visualization. The **Cartoon** effect needs to be the first to be added to the image because it doesn't blend so well with previous effects and it is great to bring more brightness and detail when using along with the effect.

Drawing with a pencil

Drawing is a method of expression within visual arts and at the same time one of the simplest and most proficient means of communicating ideas. During the preproduction stage, we may also need to produce some sketches in order to graphically demonstrate an idea or material. Lumion provides a nice effect called **Sketch** and this recipe will help you to produce both a line drawing and a colored sketch.

Getting ready

To completely understand how this effect works, remove or hide any effects you may have applied to your scene.

How to do it...

To add the **Sketch** effect to your visualization, perform the following steps:

1. From the **Movie** or **Photo** mode, use the **New effect** button to open the effects library.

2. Inside the effects library, open the **Artistic** tab and select the **Sketch** effect.

3. The default values produce a good-looking colorful sketch that per se is a good result, but let's see how you can improve this sketch and produce a line drawing.

4. Start by dragging the **Accuracy** slider to a value of **1.5** or **1.8** and you can see that by increasing this setting, your image looks sharper.

5. Next, decrease the **Sketch style** slider to a value between **0.4** and **0.8** and you can perceive that the 3D model's outlines start to fade away.

6. Use the **Contrast** slider to improve the contrast between the shadows and light and bring out the colors.

7. Increase the **Coloring** setting to not only achieve more vivid colors, but also to start bringing some colors that are not perceived when using values below **1.4** or **1.7** depending on the project.

8. The **Dynamic** setting can be used to bring randomness to your images, thereby adding and removing opacity to random points in your sketch.

9. With these settings, you can produce a colored sketch with vivid colors and a good contrast, as shown in the following screenshot:

10. To produce a line drawing, you need to set the **Sketch style** setting to the highest value, which is **2**, and you will notice that the sketch look is removed.

11. Next, completely remove all the color using the **Coloring** slider and you may want to decrease the **Contrast** setting too.

12. The **Outline fadeout** value needs to be **1** or a lower value; otherwise, as the name indicates, the outlines will start to disappear.

13. If you want a sharp look, change the **Accuracy** slider to **1.6** or higher, but if you want a more pencil-look drawing, decrease the value to **0**. The following screenshot shows the different results:

Painting with Watercolor

Watercolor is a painting technique, which uses pigments that are water soluble. There are some artists that still make amazing architectural visualizations using this technique and although it is quite different from the typical photorealistic renders, the beauty of the watercolor lies within its properties. Colors appear to glow on the paper, whereas, other pigments leave sediments into the painting, bringing uniqueness to the concept we need to deliver. Lumion does a fairly good job with the **Watercolor** effect.

Getting ready

To completely understand how this effect works, you may want to search for watercolor paintings and illustrations.

How to do it...

To apply the **Watercolor** effect, perform the following steps:

1. Go to the **Movie** or **Photo** mode.
2. To add the **Watercolor** effect, use the **New effect** button to open the effects library.
3. You can find the **Watercolor** effect in the **Artistic** tab.
4. The **Watercolor** effect is immediately applied to your image. For some artists this will be enough.
5. But let's improve the aspect of your watercolor illustration. With this effect, you can achieve several stages and styles of watercolor painting that can later be combined to achieve a more realistic look.
6. The following steps will create three different images, each one with a different style that will later be combined in Gimp or Photoshop in order to create a more complex and believable watercolor painting.
7. Let's start by blocking the color. When painting, the most efficient way to achieve a good composition and unity is to initially develop larger color areas.
8. But first, export the frame you have with the default settings and this will be the base image to start working with. You can name it `Base_` to follow this recipe.
9. Reduce the **Accuracy** setting to **0**. As you can see, this will remove some of the details, making the image blotchier.
10. The **Radial accuracy** setting can be reduced to **0** too. What this does is it removes the details on the borders of the image.
11. Remove all the depth accuracies to eliminate any details you may have in the distance, things such as mountains, other buildings, or 3D models.

12. The **Distance** setting works like a DOF and if the value is **0**, everything will be in focus, but if you begin to increase the value, the objects at a certain distance will start to appear blurred.

13. To finish blocking the color, you may want to use the **White out** slider to remove some of the color on the borders of your frame. This will work like the **Vignette** effect, but instead of darkening the corners, this will remove the color.

14. Export the image. This will be the image for your second layer and you can name it `Block_`.

15. The final image is the one where you increase the **Accuracy**, **Radial accuracy**, and **Depth accuracy** values to get the best details possible. Remove any value that you may have in the **White out** slider.

16. Use the **Dynamic** setting for a different paper texture thereby bringing uniqueness to your project, and export this final image as `Detail_`.

How it works...

You have three images now and the following screenshot shows you one possibility to place them in Gimp or Photoshop:

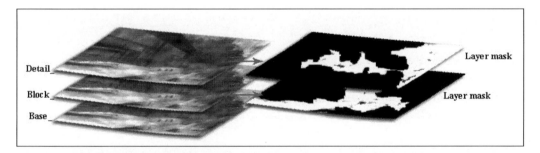

By "possibility", I mean that this is a creative and artistic process, so you should stick to one example and start exploring different possibilities.

These steps are prepared to be used in Photoshop, but the concept can be easily applied to other applications. The way this takes place is the **Base_** image stays intact and the **Block_** image uses a black layer mask to hide all the information from this layer. Then, using a brush with a white color and an opacity between 30 percent and 50 percent, we select the layer mask and start painting to add color blocking in places where we don't detail so as to distract the viewer and removing some color from the borders, reproducing the effect that this was painted on paper. We apply the same exact principle on the **Detail_** image. In this situation, our goal is to add details and color to areas where we want the viewer to focus their attention.

Creating stills

Creating a still image or static image is easy. Open the **Photo** mode, add the effects we need to improve and enrich the image, and export it. However, it may happen that we only prepared the movie clip and don't have any camera positions specified to be used in the **Photo** mode. Besides, it means that we have to spend more time to add all the effects and tweak them. Nevertheless, Lumion allows us to use the **Movie** mode to export a sequence of images or just a single image.

Getting ready

Before we begin, it is worth mentioning that in Lumion, we have the opportunity to save and load camera positions. This is primarily possible in the **Build** mode using the key combination of *Ctrl + 0, 1, 2,... 9* to save up to 10 camera positions and the key combination of *Shift + 0, 1, 2,... 9* to load the same camera positions. When in the **Photo** mode, we can see these saved camera positions on the top of the interface represented by thumbnails. In the **Photo** mode, we can change the camera position and use the same key combination to save the new position, or just use the **Store camera** button that appears below the thumbnail, as shown in the following screenshot:

How to do it...

To export a single image in the **Movie** mode, perform the following steps:

1. In the bottom-right corner of the screen, click on the **Save Movie** button.

2. This opens a new window called **Save your entire movie**, but we just want to create some static images.

3. Open the **Images** tab to access the following options:

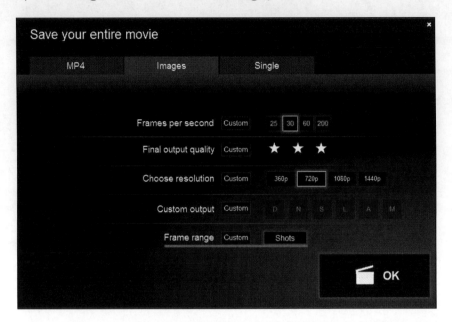

4. If you want to save a sequence of images, it is essential that you use the **Frames per second** option to export these images correctly.

5. You may want to check the **Final output quality** and **Choose resolution** settings to verify that these options have the correct settings you need.

6. You may also want to focus your attention on the **Frame range** setting. By default, the mode that is set for the frame range is **Auto**, but you also need the **Custom** mode.

7. Click on the **Auto** button and the **Custom** button appears. On the right-hand side, a second button appears called **Shots** and if you click on this button, you can cycle between the **Shots** and **Range** options.

8. Click on the **Shots** option to change from the **Shots** option to the **Range** option. Two fields will appear on the right-hand side of the screen allowing you to specify the first and last frame. If you move your mouse over each field, it will show a small preview window, which will visually tell you what image is in that frame.

9. The second option we have is directly related to the way clips are created. To create a clip, you need to record and start taking shots and then Lumion will fill the gaps between each main shot. So, when you use the **Shots** option to export the images, Lumion picks these shots and exports them. This means that if you need to take five shots to create a clip, Lumion will export five images. Keep in mind that if you have more than one clip, Lumion will export the main shots from these clips too.

10. After selecting your option, click on the **OK** button to save the images and start rendering.

Using special formats

Lumion gives us the opportunity to export different render passes. Render passes or render elements are the raw elements produced by the rendering engine that are used together to create the final image. These special formats can be extracted and combined with software that supports composition using layers. The reason why we do this is to get much greater control and tweak the look of the final image. Let's see how we can export these render passes and some of their practical applications.

Getting ready

Before we start, it is good to identify which render passes we can obtain from Lumion. We can export six render passes: **Depthmap**, **Normalmap**, **SpecularReflection map**, **Lighting map**, **Sky alpha map**, and **Material ID**.

How to do it...

To export the aforementioned render passes from Lumion, perform the following steps:

1. Go to the **Movie** mode and click on the **Save movie** button.

2. A new window will open and in order to export the render passes, you can either select the **Images** tab if you are interested in saving a sequence of images or select the **Single** tab to export an individual image.

3. Look for the **Custom output** setting to access the following settings:

4. You need to click on each letter in order to define the render passes you want to be saved along with your normal render.

5. After this, click on the **OK** button to save the images into a folder and Lumion will start rendering the passes.

How it works...

Now that we have the render passes, how can we use them? An explanation of all the details involved in using all these passes would probably fill an entire chapter, but let's have a quick overview to understand what information we can get and a brief explanation of what we can do with them, as explained in the following list:

- **(M) Material ID**: With this render pass, Lumion assigns a color to each material used in the scene. This render pass can be used in applications, such as Gimp or Photoshop, to isolate areas and tweak the colors in the image.

- **(A) Sky alpha map**: This is a black and white image that works as a mask and can be used to replace the sky with a different one or control the sky without affecting the rest of the image.

- **(D) Depthmap**: This is an image that has information of the distance of the 3D models from your camera. The most practical applications use this image to simulate fog, smoke, and DOF.

- **(N) Normalmap**: This is a regular image where the red, green, and blue colors correspond to the X, Y, and Z coordinates of the normal surface. This image can be used to change the light direction, although this is not necessary with Lumion.

- **(S) SpecularReflection map**: This is an image with information related to the surface shine and highlights color. This information can be used to make a surface appear more visually interesting, improving the reflections and also tinting the image.

- **(L) Lighting map**: This is an image with the light and brightness information for each surface in your project. This information can be useful to improve the contrast and shadows, and control the light using layer masks.

Creating and combining different NPR effects

Lumion has some splendid artistic effects that can be used to produce some technical illustration, architectural visualizations, or conceptual designs. We can use each effect individually and the outcome is still professional and with high quality. However, as we mentioned in the beginning of this chapter, making art is a creative, intelligent, and thoughtful process. Let's see the two ways in which we can use all or some of these effects to take our visualizations to the next level.

Getting ready

To use this recipe, you will need to know how to work with Gimp or Photoshop.

How to do it...

Let's define the effects you need, as shown in the following steps:

1. Apply the **Manga** effect and export two images: one with full color and another with just the outlines. You can name them `M_line` and `M_color`.

2. Next, apply the **Cartoon** effect and save an image with just the outlines as `C_line`.

3. Open these three images in a software that can work with layers, such as Gimp or Photoshop.

4. The line work produced with the **Manga** effect has clean lines with loads of information from textures beneath this effect. The **Cartoon** effect can produce a line work where the outlines are thicker, but we don't get much detail.

5. In Gimp or Photoshop, use the **M_color** image as the base for this illustration. On top of this layer, add the **C_line** and **M_line** images and change both these layers to multiply. What this does is it removes the white areas and leaves the black lines.

6. The following screenshot should give you an idea of how this process works:

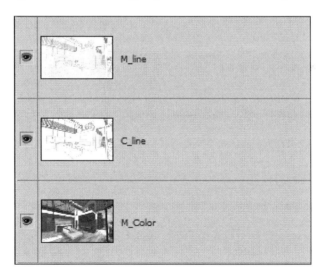

7. The following screenshot is the result you will get:

8. For the next style, you need to apply the **Sketch** effect and export an image with just the outlines and no color called S_line.

9. Apply the **Watercolor** effect and save the image as W_color.

10. In Gimp or Photoshop, use the **W_color** image as the base.

11. On top of the **W_color** image, add the **S_line** image and create a white mask.

12. The next step is to pick a brush that's black in color with an opacity of 30 percent or 50 percent, select the mask, and start painting. This means it starts adding color in places you want the viewer to focus his/her attention, as you can see in the following screenshot:

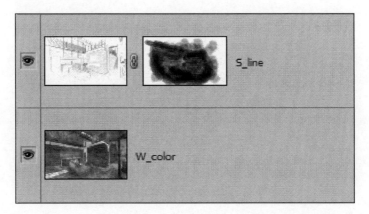

13. The final image will look like the following screenshot:

10
Bringing Your World to Life

In this chapter, we will cover the following recipes:

- ▶ Creating a camera path
- ▶ Changing clips
- ▶ Animating the 3D models
- ▶ Bringing people to life
- ▶ Controlling the camera
- ▶ Animating curved paths
- ▶ Animating the camera's focus
- ▶ Using motion blur
- ▶ Animating the layers
- ▶ Configuring the Near Clip Distance effect
- ▶ Animating effects

Introduction

Lumion is a powerful technology, and some of its strength lies in its possibility to create an amazing and astonishing walk-through visualization with simplicity and speediness that is remarkable. Lumion provides everything that is required to populate a project with high-quality models, realistic materials, and special effects. However, it is when we create an animation and export it as a video file or an image sequence that we can perceive the true power of this real-time technology. Then again, the technology by itself doesn't create beautiful and eye-catching animations; we need to master it, and this chapter is aimed to help you learn and improve your animation skills.

Creating a camera path

Creating a clip in Lumion involves using a method called camera path. In Lumion, a movie is made up of one or more clips, and each clip needs a camera path to be animated. The camera path is not a physical path that we can create and make the camera follow. Instead, the camera path is set by multiple snapshots that define the different camera positions. The **Movie** mode is where we can find the tools required to create this camera path and start bringing life to our world.

Getting ready

Before we start, just a reminder that to navigate to some of the viewports in the **Movie** mode, we need to use the same keys and mouse buttons that we use in the **Build** mode. As an aide memoire, the following are some of the most used shortcuts to navigate in Lumion:

- *WSAD* or arrow keys: These move the camera forward, backward, or to the left or right
- *Q*: This moves the camera upward
- *E*: This moves the camera downward
- Spacebar + *WSAD* and *QE*: These slow down the camera speed
- *Shift* + *WSAD* and *QE*: These increase the camera speed
- *Shift* + Spacebar + *WSAD* and *QE*: This is an option to choose a high-speed camera
- Press the right mouse button and move it to look around
- Press the middle mouse button and move the mouse to pan

How to do it...

Let's start by accessing the **Movie** mode with the following steps:

1. On the right-hand side of the screen, find the **Movie** mode button symbolized by a movie clip icon.

2. This opens a new interface that is quite different from the **Build** mode. The recipes in this chapter will cover other aspects of this interface; for now, we are going to focus on the section at the bottom of the screen, which is shown in the following screenshot:

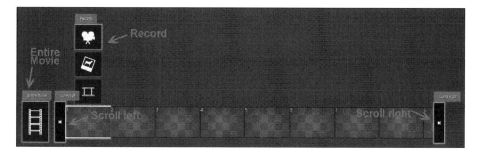

3. The movie bar contains all the clips created, and when an empty clip is selected, three options appear over the clip that is selected.

4. The first option is the one we need to create or record a camera path, so click on this button and again a new window appears, as shown in the following screenshot:

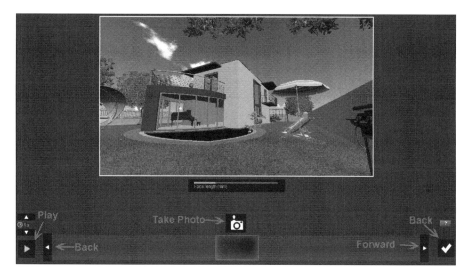

5. The fun starts now because recording a camera path is as easy as taking a snapshot, then moving the camera and taking another snapshot, and so on.

6. First, start by moving the camera to a location where you want to start your animation.

7. With the camera placed at the correct position, click on the **Take Photo** option to take a snapshot, which will be saved in the lower bar. This will be the start of your video.

8. Move the camera to another place in your scene and take another snapshot.

9. Repeat step 8 until you are satisfied with the camera path that you have created.

10. To preview the animation you just created, click on the **Play** button; this will start playing the video in loops, and you need to click on the **Play** button again to pause the video.

11. To finish the animation, click on the **Back** button, which is represented by a check mark and placed at the bottom-right corner of the screen.

12. Back in the movie interface, you can select another clip and repeat the process to record another animation.

How it works...

When taking a photo, we are actually keyframing the camera's position, and Lumion fills the gaps between each snapshot, thus creating an animation. The amount of snapshots we take will dictate the size of the clip. As a reference, each snapshot you create is equal to 2 seconds of animation.

Changing clips

Creating a camera path is the initial step to produce incredible walk-through visualizations. However, it is difficult to create a perfect animation at the initial attempt; as a result, it is natural that we need to tweak the camera positions, delete some sections to produce a more flowing movement, or even change the camera speed. These alterations are part of the process to produce a video, and Lumion allows us to introduce these modifications with great simplicity. Let's see how we can do that.

Getting ready

Sometimes, the modifications we need to make are fairly simple; perhaps, the most common modification will be fine-tuning the position of the camera. The best way to control Lumion's camera is by slowing down the camera speed using the following hotkeys:

▸ Spacebar + *WSAD* and *QE*: Using this combination of keys, you can slow down the camera speed

How to do it...

To change a clip, perform the following steps:

1. On the right-hand side of the screen, locate and select the **Movie** mode button if you are not in the **Movie** mode already.

2. Select a clip with an animation and you will be offered two methods to edit the clip. On the top-left corner of the screen, you have the **Edit clip** button, which is represented with a camera icon. You can use this method or double-click on the clip to edit it.

3. Select the **Edit clip** button and the window that appears is the same that you used to create the initial camera path. Back in this window, you again have different possibilities to edit the clip.

4. The first option is to edit the camera's position; for this, you need to select the thumbnail that represents the camera's position, and using the viewport above this thumbnail, you can adjust the camera to a new position.

5. After this, it is essential that you click on the **Take Photo** button that now has a reload icon, as you can see in the following screenshot:

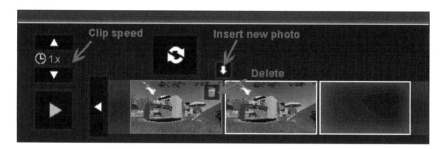

6. There are two more ways to edit the clip and they are highlighted in the previous screenshot. The first is the opportunity to delete or remove a camera position.

7. The second option to edit the animation is the possibility to accurately control the camera's speed, and consequently, influence the length of the animation. This means that if you increase the speed, the animation will be shorter, and according to the same principle, when you reduce the speed, the animation becomes longer.

8. Above the **Play** button, you can find the two buttons that permit you to increase or decrease the speed of the clip. Lumion gives you a hand by informing you about the new length of the animation every time you click on those buttons.

9. After editing the clip, click on the **Back** button to return to the **Movie** mode.

Animating the 3D models

Lumion's animation tools can transport our walk-through to the next level because after we create a walk-through, we have an opportunity to animate individual 3D models. It is true that we can import animations in Lumion, but these imported animations are tricky to control and need to be carefully planned. On the other hand, Lumion has tools that we need to animate the native 3D models and add life to our world. Let's see how we can do that.

Getting ready

To apply this recipe, it is essential that we have at least one clip that is animated, and this animation needs to encompass the 3D models we want to animate. All of the animation process is done in the **Movie** mode, so we need to place the 3D models before using the **Movie** mode.

How to do it...

With the **Movie** mode open, perform the following steps:

1. First, create a clip if necessary or select the clip you want to animate.

2. Click on the **New effect** button, and from the **Movie effect** library, open the **Objects** tab.

3. Select the **Move** effect. It is one of the simplest effects to animate a 3D model, and for this example, you can animate a car.

4. A new module is applied to your movie interface, and you need to select the button with the pencil icon to start animating objects.

5. Click on the button and the interface changes to a sort of **Build** mode, but the only tools available are as shown in the following screenshot:

6. Animating 3D models using this tool is really simple because you only have to define the start and end position.

7. First of all, click on the **Start position** button and then using the available tools such as **Move**, **Move vertical**, **Rotate**, **Size**, and other rotate options, adjust the 3D model's position.

8. As the next step, click on the **End position** button, and after that, define the final position. It is important that you follow these steps in this order, otherwise your animation will be wrong.

9. To change the animation, you need to follow the same steps again. First, select the **Start position** or **End position** buttons and then make the necessary adjustments.

10. To finalize the animation, click on the **Back** button.

How it works...

The process is very simple and again uses the concept of using keyframes to specify the initial and last positions. The **Move** effect is the best option when we need to animate an object going from point A to point B in a straight line. However, we need to keep in mind that if the the clip has, for example, 12 seconds, it will take 12 seconds for the car or other 3D model to travel the path that is defined, even if the path is just 1 meter long.

Bringing people to life

Lumion presents us with the opportunity to boost architectural visualizations by introducing animated people. We can bring a walk-through to a professional level by using animated people walking around buildings and other elements in our project. Going from point A to point B in a straight line is easy and it can be done using the **Move** effect, but things start to get complicated when we need to animate a person on a more complex path. Let's see how we can create more complex animations using Lumion.

Getting ready

Before we start, it is good to remember that there is a difference between an animated person and a person involved in a walk cycle. The first type is an idle element, but with a loop animation. The second type of person is the one we need for this recipe, and as soon as we place them in the scene, they start walking without actually moving. This is why we need to use the **Advanced move** effect.

How to do it...

To create more complex animations, perform the following steps:

1. From the **Movie** mode, select the clip that contains the 3D models you want to animate.

2. Click on the **New effect** button, and from the **Objects** tab, select the **Advanced move** effect.

3. A new module is added to the movie mode interface, and to start animating, you need to click on the button with a pencil icon.

4. The interface for this effect is slightly different from that of the **Move** effect, as shown in the following screenshot:

5. Instead of buttons to delineate the start and end position, you have the **Time** bar that represents the length of your clip, and using the left mouse button, you can start scrubbing along the bar to stipulate the time for a specific position, rotation, or scale.

6. For example, at 0 seconds, you want the person to be at point A, then at 5 seconds, the person needs to be at point B, and at 10 seconds, it will stop at point C. Let's see this in a practical way.

7. First, make sure that the **Time** bar is at **0** seconds.

8. Then, by means of the tools available, adjust the position of the 3D model and a small white line with a dot appears on the **Time** bar; this shows that you keyframed the position, the rotation, or the scale of that 3D model.

9. To create the initial keyframe, you need to make at least a small adjustment; otherwise, Lumion will not create a keyframe. It may happen that once you make that small adjustment, the person or other 3D model will change its orientation. Don't worry; it will work out fine in the end.

10. Drag the bar for a few seconds later and move the person to a different location. By doing this, another keyframe is defined, as you can see in the following screenshot:

11. For the rest of the path, repeat step 8 until you are satisfied with the result.

12. You can also increase or decrease the length of the clip using the buttons on the left-hand side of the screen, and this is done by adding or removing seconds from the animation. Sometimes 5 seconds may be enough for a car to move from one point to another, but a person walking will take longer.

13. To finish the animation, click on the **Back** button.

14. Back in the **Movie** mode, there is an additional way to control the animation that is created. This setting is the **Time offset** option, and it permits you to manage time when the animation starts or offset the animation in time without having to adjust the length of your clip or rebuild the animation.

15. Using the *Shift* key, we can start to increase this value, and looking at the viewport, we will notice how the person or the 3D model starts to move. This means you can delay when the animation starts during the clip, or on the other hand, you can fast forward the animation to a specific position in the timeline.

16. A word of caution if you use the **Time offset** setting. When you try to edit the animation again, remember that the **Time** bar represents the length of the clip and not the extent of your animation. Therefore, to avoid problems, it is better to change the **Time offset** value to **0** before editing the animation, and once any correction is made, the value you had is applied automatically.

There's more...

The **Advanced move** effect is a feature that we can use with any 3D model from Lumion, such as cars, boats, airplanes, birds, and other objects. It is a powerful effect to create more complex animations, but the only thing we should avoid while doing the animation is creating a path with right angles. This happens when the 3D model needs to change its direction, such as a car changing its direction, and without thinking about it, we create a path with a right angle. This right angle will create a weird animation, so we should try to achieve a path like the one shown on the left-hand side of the following screenshot:

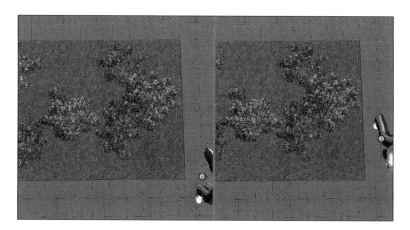

Controlling the camera

Creating a camera path is something that is fairly simple and intuitive. The controls that we use to record a camera path are the same we use in the **Build** mode. However, there are some tricks we can apply in order to direct the camera more accurately and that can make all the difference between having a clumsy, dull clip and a precise and well-directed movie. This recipe is going to help you learn some simple yet important features in order to control the camera more perfectly.

Getting ready

Before beginning this recipe, we have to store some great camera angles in the **Build** mode using the key combination *Ctrl + 0, 1, 2,* to *9* because we are going to use this feature. The idea for this recipe is to first use an initial camera position to start the animation; then, you move the camera to a second position and zoom in; and finally, you move the camera to a third position, zoom out, and finish the shot by leveling the camera.

How to do it...

Let's start by opening the **Movie** mode and performing the following steps:

1. Select a blank clip and start recording a camera path.

2. To create a camera zooming effect, you need to use the **Focal length (mm)** option, as you can see in the following screenshot:

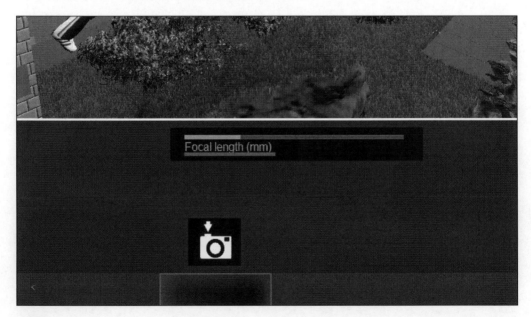

3. The value by default is **15**, but you can adjust this value up and down to create a zoom effect.

4. Load the first camera position using the key combination *Shift + 0, 1, 2, 3,* to *9* and use the **Take Photo** button to take a snapshot; however, leave the **Focal length (mm)** option with the default value.

5. Load the second camera position and adjust the **Focal length (mm)** value to a higher value in order to zoom in and take another snapshot.

6. Finally, you can load the third camera position and adjust the **Focal length (mm)** value to a lower value to zoom out.

7. Finish the camera path by leveling the camera pitch using the key combination *Ctrl + H*, and take the final snapshot.

How it works...

While placing 3D models and organizing the scene, there will be occasions when we will get a nice camera angle, and the opportunity we will have to save and load camera positions can be a time saver when producing a movie.

Zooming the camera in and out is also a simple feature, but well-placed camera zooms can make the difference between a regular movie and an attractive movie. The trick is to use camera effects such as DOF along with camera zooming; this can really enhance your walk-through.

Another fine feature when recording a movie is the grid that appears when you start to move and control the camera, as shown in the following screenshot:

This grid can be used to help us set up a rule of thirds. The principle behind the rule of thirds is to divide an image into nine equal parts. This grid now identifies four important parts of the image, as we can see are highlighted in the previous screenshot, that we should consider as placing points of interest; the four lines are also useful positions for the elements in our frame.

Animating curved paths

When we comprehend how animation works in Lumion and observe how simple the **Move** and **Advanced move** effects are, it is easy to start considering some practical and helpful applications. This recipe is initially going to cover a practical example using the **Move** effect and then cover the **Advanced move** effect in more depth. It will also tell us how to create curved paths. Two examples will be used to illustrate the true potential of this Lumion feature and how complex our walk-through visualizations can become.

Getting ready

For the first example, we are going to animate a door-opening scene. To do this, we need to import two separate files: one with the house and the second with the door. This is because the door needs to be a separate object in order to be animated separately from the house. For the second example, we are going to animate a car to exemplify how powerful the **Advanced move** effect can be and how to create complex animations using curved paths.

How to do it...

Let's start with the first example using the following steps:

1. To start, place the house and the door in your scene.

2. Go to the **Movie** mode and create a simple clip in which you make the camera go through the door. Don't forget that you need to have enough time for the door to open.

3. Apply the **Move** effect and start building a new animation.

4. Click on the **Start position** button and then using the rotate tool, close the door. Even if the door is already closed, you need to make at least a small adjustment in the rotation so that Lumion can keyframe that information.

5. The next step is to use the **End position** button to define when the door will be fully open, and then using the rotate tool, delineate the final rotation angle.

6. Use the **Play** button to verify whether the animation is correct and also if you need to modify the camera path in order to have enough time to go through the open door.

This is, in fact, a combination of two animations. In the first instance, we created a clip where the camera goes through the door, and the second animation was done using the **Move** effect. It is a simple animation, but it makes all the difference between having a movie where the camera just crosses the door and the visual impact of the door that opens and shows a beautiful exterior or a stunning living room. Moreover, this is just one example of how we can use the **Move** effect to add a special touch to our architectural visualization.

The next animation is a little bit more complex. This example is going to illustrate how we can animate a car performing a U turn, but the principles used here can easily be applied to other 3D models. This is perhaps the best way to cover how **Advanced move** works in more depth. Let's make this scene very simple; open a new scene and place a car from the Lumion library, and we can start from there by performing the following steps.

1. After creating a clip with this 3D model in the frame, add the **Advanced move** effect.

2. The best way to animate using this effect is by defining the start and end positions.

3. Select the move tool and adjust the car's location to set the first keyframe, and using the **Time** bar, go to the end of the clip and keyframe the last position, as shown in the following screenshot:

4. The previous screenshot shows that we can keyframe not only the car's position, but also the rotation, which in this case is essential. These two keyframes help you establish the initial and final position of the car, but it is not enough because now if you play the animation, the car will travel in a straight line.

5. The next keyframe you need will establish where the car will turn to go in the opposite direction.

6. Drag the **Time** bar to the middle of the clip and adjust the car's position and rotation angle.

7. Let's say, for example, you notice that the new car's position and rotation is wrong or it should be further in the **Time** bar. Unfortunately, in this scenario, you can select the keyframe and move up and down on the **Time** bar, but you cannot delete it and start again.

8. To delete a keyframe, put your mouse over the keyframe in the **Time** bar and a delete button will appear above the keyframe, as shown in the following screenshot:

9. Create another keyframe and play the animation to check how the animation looks in real time. Something may look excellent when scrubbing the **Time** bar, but it is when you play the animation that you can see whether there is a need for further adjustments.

10. It needs adjustments because using just three keyframes is not enough in this situation to create a fluid animation. However, how do you know where to put the next keyframe? Have a look at the following screenshot:

11. When you hover the mouse over any keyframe, a red dot appears on the path that is traced showing you where the keyframe is. This is particularly useful when you have several keyframes close to one another, and this feature helps you identify the correct keyframe before modifying or deleting it.

12. You may want to add two more keyframes as shown in the previous screenshot to assure that the car performs a smooth U turn.

13. Play the animation to verify whether you need additional keyframes and click on the **Back** button to save the animation.

There's more...

When we need to create this sort of animation, such as opening a door, it is usually a good idea to create a single and specific clip just for the animation. The reason why we would want to do this is because it is easier to control the animation, and if necessary, we can control the speed of the animation without interfering with the rest of the movie.

Animating the camera's focus

Creating a movie in Lumion is a straightforward task, but if we stop at the basics, the result we get is nothing particularly amazing and dazzling. It is when we start adding different elements to the equation that our animation starts to grow in quality. Some of the previous recipes in this chapter covered how to create a camera path and how to improve the camera control while recording the shot. Now it is time to start complementing those recipes with some effects. Let's see how we can add a focus effect to our camera.

Getting ready

For this recipe, we just need a very simple camera path where the camera zooms in, focuses at some object in the scene, and then moves away performing a zoom out.

How to do it...

Let's start by adding a **Depth of Field** effect to the clip by performing the following steps:

1. From the **Movie** mode, select a clip and click on the **New effect** button.

2. Open the **Camera** tab and select the **Depth of Field** effect. If you need to understand better or recall how this effect works, check the *Separating objects with DOF* recipe in *Chapter 8, Getting Realism with Camera Effects*.

3. To use this effect, you need to know when the camera starts to zoom in and when it starts to zoom out because you are using this information to step the **Depth of Field** effect.

4. There is no secret formula to using this effect and mimicking a camera zoom, so you will need to test and tweak the settings. It is always good to start with the **Focus distance** setting, and then once the object is slightly in focus, use the **F stop** setting to increase the sharpness.

5. Adjust the following settings to put your object out of focus with a blurred background; after doing this, keyframe these values using the **Create keyframe** button, as shown in the following screenshot:

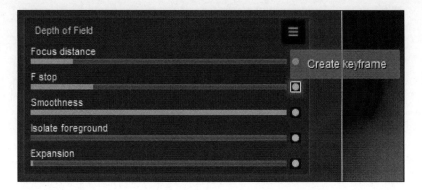

6. Move the **Time** bar for when the camera starts to use a zoom in and create another keyframe to tweak the settings.

7. Here, you need to tweak the same two values, **Focus distance** and **F stop**, to focus on the 3D model, but at the same time, trying to blur the background. This will create an effect called **Bokeh**.

8. Before the camera starts to zoom out, add another keyframe so that you can constrain the time during which the 3D model will be in focus.

9. Then, when the camera returns to the original position or to another position that you have defined, create another keyframe and adjust the settings.

How it works...

When we create a camera path, in particular, when we use the **Focal length (mm)** setting to perform zoom in and out actions, we need to use this **Depth of Field** effect to reproduce what happens in real life. This gives us freedom to play with the focus feature, allowing us to produce beautiful compositions where we can focus on a 3D model that is far and moving for a 3D model closer to the camera. The CG movie, The Third & The Seventh, by Alex Roman is a good example of this feature in action.

There's more...

This recipe covered how we can imitate the focus of a camera using the **Depth of Field** effect, but it also helped us create a beautiful effect that is called Bokeh. Bokeh comes from a Japanese word that literally means blur and it refers to the quality of an out-of-focus area in a photograph or a movie. For this recipe, we used the **Depth of Field** effect to create a shallow DOF and a blurred background. However, Bokeh is the quality of that blurred background and the reflected points of light that appear in the shot. It looks something like the following screenshot:

Why use this effect in a movie? We don't have to, but when we use the Bokeh effect, this will transform our animation into a visually interesting movie, helping the viewers to focus their attention on a particular area.

What is a good Bokeh? It is difficult to define what is considered a good or bad Bokeh, but a good Bokeh delights the eyes and our perception of the picture. Therefore, we should avoid hard edges and instead aim to create a soft and velvety blurred background with smooth round circles of light.

Using motion blur

In real life, when we take a photograph, that image doesn't represent an instant of time. The time it takes to take a photograph is defined by the exposure's setting, and in most of the situations, the exposure is enough to create a sharp image. However, when we have objects moving or a longer exposure, this creates some blurred artifacts and these artifacts are what we call motion blur. We can apply the same effect in Lumion while creating an animation or a camera path, and this recipe will show us how.

Getting ready

It is essential that you have at least a small clip to apply this effect; although, you can apply the same effect in the **Photo** mode.

How to do it...

With the **Movie** mode open, perform the following steps:

1. Select a clip and add a new effect using the **New effect** button.

2. Open the **Camera** tab and click on the **Motion blur** effect.

3. An effect as simple as this is impossible because you only have one setting to adjust, that is, **Motion blur**.

4. To see this effect on the viewport, you need to drag the clip bar a little bit forward in time and start adjusting this effect.

5. The good thing with this effect is that you don't need to keyframe the settings for when the camera starts to move and when it stops. Lumion automatically knows when to use this effect, as you can see in the following screenshot:

6. In the previous screenshot, the image on the left-hand side demonstrates that when the camera is static, the amount of motion blur is barely visible, while the image on the right-hand side shows that the camera moving and you can perceive the motion blur.

There's more...

Motion blur is frequently employed to convey a sense of speed and this is noticeable when we have an architectural visualization in a city with loads of cars and people walking in public spaces. Another benefit of using motion blur is it will make our movie look more natural and smoother.

Animating the layers

The amount of control we have over animating 3D models in Lumion is extended with the use of layers. Lumion has two effects that give us a basic control over the layers we use to organize the project, and these layers can be used to create some interesting animations. The way we are going to organize the layers depend on what we are trying to accomplish, and after this recipe, we will have a better idea of what is necessary. Let's see how we can use the **Show layer** and **Hide layer** effects.

Getting ready

Before we start this recipe, we need at least two elements. We need some 3D models placed in the scene and we need those 3D models in different layers.

How to do it...

To animate layers in Lumion, perform the following steps:

1. Select the clip with the 3D models and use the **New effect** button to open the **Movie effect** library.

2. Open the **Objects** tab, and you can start by adding the **Hide layer** effect first.

3. The **Hide layer** effect is unique in a sense that with it, you can apply more than one module to the interface and control several layers at once.

4. When you apply this effect to your project, everything you have on the first layer will be hidden.

5. Start by dragging the slider, and if you have 3D models in each layer when you move the slider to the right-hand side of the bar, the objects in the first layer will appear; the 3D models in the second layer will disappear if you have 3D models in the second layer.

6. You can control up to 20 layers in Lumion with this effect.

7. The second effect to control layers is by using the other effect called **Show layers** that you can find in the **Objects** tab.

8. Add this effect to your clip, and this effect will work differently on some points.

9. Drag the slider to change the layers, and contrary to the previous effect, this will only show the layer that is selected. While the **Hide layer** effect will hide a layer, all the other layers will be visible; however, with the **Show layer** effect, only the layer selected will be visible.

10. With this effect, you can animate the effects and keyframe the different layers and also control when they should appear.

There's more...

Why should we use this effect? It really depends on what type of visualization we are working on, but these effects can and are used to create movies, which is the main purpose to present information regarding a construction detail and how spaces inside buildings look with and without furniture. The **Show layer** and **Hide layer** effects can be used together to optimize Lumion's performance while rendering movies. When a scene is too big and starts to affect the render time, we can use these effects to organize different sections of the project and when they should appear and disappear in front of the camera.

Configuring the Near Clip Distance effect

This next feature can be used to add both an object and an effect to our scene. In the first instance, we can go to the **Objects** menu in the **Build** menu and find this feature under the **Lights and special objects** submenu. Almost the same feature can be applied and animated using the **Near Clip Distance** effect as we are going to see in this recipe. We are also going to see why this effect will be useful while producing technical or conceptual illustrations.

Getting ready

To understand this effect in a better way, we can add any house from the Lumion library. We can also create a small clip where the camera path is going through a house and we will see why. This effect can also be used in the **Photo** mode.

How to do it...

To add the **Near Clip Distance** effect to one of your clips, perform the following steps:

1. Select the clip and using the **New effect** button, add the **Near Clip Distance** effect.

2. This effect can be found under the **Camera** tab.

3. Start adjusting the **Near clip plane** setting to control the clip plane.

4. If you follow the guidelines provided in the *Getting ready* section of this recipe, you should get an animation that looks like the following screenshot once you apply this effect:

5. This effect creates a plane that will clip any 3D model in front of the camera, and the **Near clip plane** setting controls how far that clip can go.

There's more...

At first glance, we may think why do we need this effect and this is not useful at all. It is true that this effect is not something that we are going to use in every single project. Usually, the client will want an exterior or interior image, and if they want a movie, it will be a walk-through showing the house. However, some projects may require us to produce what is called an bird's-eye view, and the main goal here is to show the different spaces inside the building and how they work together. The **Near Clip Distance** effect can then be used to show the floors and how they are organized with furniture and other elements, but we can unlock the full potential of this effect when we animate this effect; without moving the camera, it is possible to show all the floors of a small house.

Animating effects

This recipe is not about any special feature or secret to animate effects. Instead, this recipe will work as an exercise to illustrate how we can animate different effects and how those effects when combined can transport any walk-through that we may produce to the next level. For this recipe, we will make use of the **Sun study**, **Cloud**, and **Rain** effects.

Getting ready

For this exercise, we need a small clip, and using the **Sun study**, **Cloud**, and **Rain** effects, we are going to create a transition between a sunny day and a rainy day.

How to do it...

Let's start by adding some effects by performing the following steps:

1. Select the clip with the animation and use the **New effect** button.

2. From the **World** tab, select the **Sun study** effect. To better understand how this effect works, have a look at the *Using the Sun study effect* recipe in *Chapter 5, Controlling the Weather*.

3. The first step towards using this effect is selecting a location using the button with the pencil icon, although this is not required for this example.

4. After selecting a location, we can create and keyframe some settings in this effect to produce a more interesting look. For demonstration purposes, we want a sunny day until the middle of the clip, then the clouds to darken little by little, and eventually arrive at the moment when it starts to rain.

5. Move the clip bar to the beginning of the animation and create a keyframe for the **Hour** setting, as shown in the following screenshot:

6. We are going to keyframe the **Hour** setting to create a time-lapse effect, so adjusting the setting to **8** will show 8 a.m.

7. Move the clip bar to the middle of the animation and create a keyframe for the **Hour** setting with a value of **15**. Now, if you play the animation, the sun will keep moving in the sky and the shadows on the ground create this feeling of a time-lapse effect.

8. To improve this animation, add the **Cloud** effect that can be found in the **Weather** tab.

9. Now, you are going to animate the clouds that will move in the sky. For this, you may want to create a keyframe for the **Position** setting in the beginning and in the middle of the animation. The values you can use are just a matter of taste, but try to synchronize the speed of the shadows with the speed of the clouds.

10. Play the animation to check whether the effects need any further adjustment. Remember that if you need to delete any keyframe, use the arrows above the setting to navigate between keyframes and then delete the keyframe using the **Remove keyframe** button, as shown in the following screenshot:

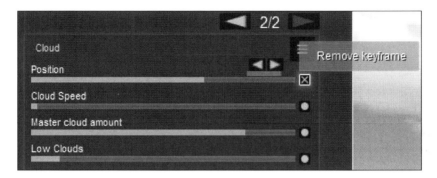

11. The next step is to create the transition between a sunny day and a rainy day, and for that, you need to add the **Rain** effect found under the **Weather** tab.

12. Play the animation and you can see that the entire clip is affected by the **Rain** effect. This means that you need to define when the **Rain** effect should start taking effect.

13. To define when the **Rain** effect starts, you need to know where the **Sun study** and **Cloud** effects have their keyframes.

14. Hover the mouse over the setting that is animated, and on the clip bar, you will see some small white lines that represent the keyframes created, as represented in the following screenshot:

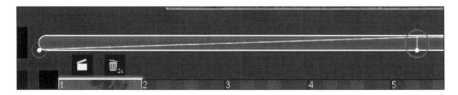

15. Using this method, verify where the **Sun study** effect's last keyframe is, move the clip bar close to this keyframe, and jump to the **Rain** effect.

16. Set a value of **0** for the **Rain density** and **Cloudy** settings, and this will remove any rain from the scene; don't forget to create a keyframe.

17. Then, drag the clip bar a few seconds further and create a keyframe with the same settings, but only change the **Cloudy** value so that the clouds start to appear darker.

18. Move a little bit further in the clip bar and create a keyframe for the **Rain density** setting so the rain will start falling.

19. Play the animation and now you can see the sunny day being transformed into a rainy day. However, look again; there is something wrong with the clip.

20. The fact is that even after using the **Rain** effect or the **Snow** effect, the sun still affects the scene and produces strong shadows.

21. To solve this issue, click on the **New effect** button, and under the **World** tab, select the **Sun** effect. This **Sun** effect will not interfere with the **Sun study** effect that was used previously.

22. To eliminate the shadows, you need to remove the **Sun brightness** effect from the **Sun** effect.

23. If you follow steps 15 and 16 of this recipe, you should have two keyframes for the **Cloudy** setting. Using these keyframes as a guideline, you can synchronize the clouds getting darker and at the same time decrease the **Sun brightness** setting, thus making the day darker and removing the shadows.

24. Play the animation; now your clip has a perfect transition between a sunny and rainy day.

11
Creating Videos

In this chapter, we will cover the following recipes:

- Affecting individual clips
- Affecting the entire video
- Handling the clips
- Creating transitions
- Camera effects
- Using the Titles effect
- Framing and composition
- Adding sound

Introduction

Now, we enter the stage where we need to present the project that we have been working on so arduously. All the hard work of sculpting the terrain, changing the landscape textures, adding a variety of 3D models, and animations are useless if we don't have the means to connect them with the viewer and show the project and the idea. If an image is worth a thousand words, imagine how many words we can get with 25 images per second.

This chapter is going to pick up some elements of the previous chapters and combine them in a way that they produce not only beautiful, but also interesting movies. We will start with some useful information to have a better control over the clips and make good use of them, mentioning some effects that can add a special touch and finalizing some tips and techniques that can really transform the way we produce a movie.

Affecting individual clips

Building a camera path is the first step to produce a decent clip, and usually, the next phase is of adding effects to that clip in order to improve the animation that is created. This recipe introduces some techniques to add effects to individual clips and how they can contribute to have a smoother workflow.

Getting ready

To follow this recipe, we need at least one clip, although two clips will help us understand some techniques that are demonstrated in a better way.

How to do it...

To apply effects to individual clips, perform the following steps:

1. Go to the **Movie** mode and, if necessary, create two simple clips.

2. To add an effect to a clip, you need to select it first; you know that the clip is selected because a halo will appear around the clip and two buttons appear on top of the clip.

3. On the top-left corner of the screen, you can find at least four buttons, as shown in the following screenshot:

4. To add an effect, select the **New effect** button and the **Movie effect** window appears, giving you access to six different categories.

5. The six categories are shown in the following screenshot:

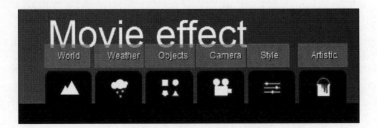

6. Then, open a tab and click on any effect with the left mouse button to select the effect and add it to the movie interface. Add a few more effects to this clip.

7. As you have a second clip, it makes sense that some of the effects that you applied and tweaked in the first clip be used in the second clip as well, avoiding the effort of tweaking the same effects again and again.

8. To do this, we need to use the **Copy** button that is next to the **New effect** button.

9. Click on this button and all the effects used on a specific clip are copied to the Lumion memory. There is another button called **Paste** that appears next to the **Copy** button, as you can see in the following screenshot:

10. This feature is very flexible as you will see in the following steps.

11. Select another clip and click on the **Paste** button. Once you do this, all the effects are applied to the clip.

12. Open the **Photo** mode and click on the **Paste** button and again all the effects used in the clip can be applied to this mode too.

13. You can also use this feature to clean the applied effects from the clips instead of having to manually delete every effect.

14. Select a clip without effects, click on the **Copy** button and paste it on the clip with effects to remove them, and start from scratch.

Affecting the entire video

The amount of control we have over each individual clip gives us the opportunity to tweak specific requirements and add a character to each clip. This also means that we need to add effects to each individual clip, and in some situations, copy and paste the same effect from other clips. Lumion give us the opportunity to go higher in the hierarchy and control the entire movie and the effects we can add. Let's see how we can control an entire video.

Getting ready

For this recipe, we will need at least one clip in the **Movie** mode.

How to do it...

Let's see how easy it is to control an entire video; this can be done by performing the following steps:

1. Go to the **Movie** mode and create one or more clips.

2. When you open the **Movie** mode, by default, you start working with the clips, which makes sense because you need at least one clip to create a video.

3. To combine all the clips in one single movie, on the left-hand side below the **Play** button, locate and click on the **Entire Movie** button, as shown in the following screenshot:

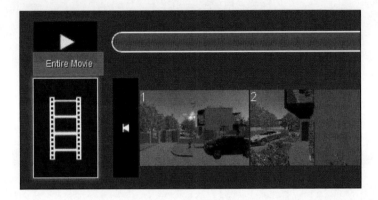

4. Apparently, nothing changes in the interface, but look again! You will see that after clicking on the **Entire Movie** button, the clip bar now encompasses all the clips in your project; also, the divisions on the bar represent the space that each clip takes, as you can see in the following screenshot:

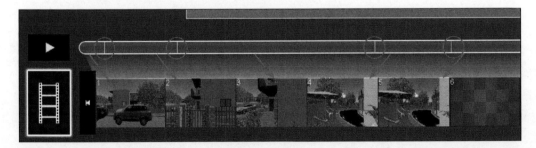

5. If you want to edit or change a clip, simply select the clip and you will be back to the clip mode.

6. The advantage of using the **Entire Movie** option is that it offers the possibility to add effects to all the clips at once, and this makes sense when there is an effect that is common to all the clips.

7. To add an effect, just click on the **New effect** button on the top-left corner of the screen and you will see that some effects, such as the **Global Illumination** and **Foliage wind** effects, aren't available.

8. Open the **Objects** tab and you will see that you have access to a new effect called **Sound**; if you open the **Camera** tab, there is another new effect called **Stereoscopic settings** but you can only use it in the WAV file format.

9. Select a new effect to add to the entire movie. After doing this, if you play the movie, you will see that the effect is applied to all the clips and not to individual clips. This means that if you had applied the **Sun study** effect to the movie, when you select an individual clip, this effect is not present.

How it works...

You may be curious to know about the **Stereoscopic settings** effect. It is an effect that lets you export a movie in a special format that when reproduced and seen with 3D glasses gives you the impression that it lends more depth to the movie.

Handling the clips

A movie is made up of several different clips; consequently, a key point at this stage is the way we will manage and organize these clips. An organized project as well as some useful habits will help us improve our workflow and ensure that our creativity isn't constrained by the lack of management and control over the clips in the project. Let's see some best practices to control the clips.

Getting ready

For this recipe, we need to have two clips created in the **Movie** mode.

How to do it...

After opening the **Movie** mode, perform the following steps:

1. Create two small clips just as an example for this recipe; alternatively, you can use any Lumion's scene from the **Examples** tab.

2. As mentioned in the previous recipe, in order to combine these two clips and add effects to both of them, click on the **Entire Movie** button in the bottom-left corner of the screen.

3. Click on the **Play** button and all the clips you have created are combined in one single movie, giving you the opportunity to add effects to all the clips in one go.

4. After creating a clip, you have an opportunity to rename it because by default, the name assigned is the clip number with the flythrough attached.

5. To rename the clip, select it and on the top-left corner of the screen is a line of text that you can edit to give it a different name, as shown in the following screenshot:

6. Create a third clip to exemplify how you can edit the clips by rearranging them.

7. To change the order of your clips, you need to select and drag the clip with the left mouse button, and when you do that, an arrow will show where you can place the clip that is selected, as shown in the following screenshot:

8. Every time you select a clip, two buttons will appear on top of the clip, as shown in the following screenshot:

9. The **Create movie from clip** button allows you to save individual clips instead of an entire movie when using the **Save Movie** button.

10. The **Remove clip** button if clicked twice deletes the clip.

These are some tips for working in a better way with the clips created, and all of the techniques covered in this chapter can also be applied to other types of clips in Lumion. When you select an empty clip, Lumion gives you three options to create a clip. The first is when we record the camera path, the second is creating a clip by importing an image, and the third option is importing a video file. Let's see how we can use the last two options to create clips using the following steps:

1. Select a blank clip and click on the **Image** button.

2. This will open a new window where you can navigate to the folder that contains the image you want to import.

3. Select the image and a 5-second clip is created with the image attached.

4. You can change the length of the clip, replace the image with another file, and add effects using the buttons on the top-left corner of the screen, as you can see in the following screenshot:

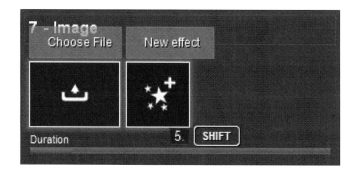

5. Add a new effect using the **New effect** button and the **Movie effect** library appears, giving you access only to the **Style** and **Artistic** tabs.

6. Get back to the **Movie** mode, select another blank clip, and click on the **Movie from file** button; however, keep in mind that you can only import MP4 files.

7. The options available to control this clip are the same except that you cannot control the length of the clip like you did with the image.

8. You can only add effects from the **Style** and **Artistic** tabs.

Creating transitions

Dissolve is a film technique that is used to create a gradual transition from one image or scene to another. The expressions "fade-out" and "fade-in" are used to describe this transition that can be used to suggest the passage of time and to change from one scene to the next. The same technique can be used in Lumion; it allows us to create smooth transitions between clips.

Getting ready

To apply the **In/out** effect, we need at least one clip, and two clips if we want to create a transition between clips.

How to do it...

To create transitions between clips, perform the following steps:

1. Open the **Movie** mode and create two small clips.
2. Select the first clip and add a new effect using the **New effect** button.
3. In the **Movie effect** library, locate the **Style** tab and select the **In/out** effect.
4. This will add a new module to the interface with these settings available, as shown in the following screenshot:

5. Fade-in and fade-out typically have a duration of 1 to 2 seconds and that is controlled using the **In duration(s)** and **Out duration(s)** settings.
6. If you are using this effect to create a transition between clips, you need to add this effect to both the clips and change the duration on each one to **0.5** instead of **1**, unless you want a transition of 2 seconds.
7. The next step will be to choose the type of transition you want. As you can see in the previous screenshot, there are four types of transitions available: **Black**, **White**, **Blur**, and **Black Blur**.
8. The best way to see whether the effect is producing a good transition or not and whether the effect is applied to both the clips is by clicking on the **Entire movie** button.

There's more...

The length of the dissolve effect is dictated by the mood we want to accomplish. For instance, in the opening sequence of a movie, the initial fade-in can be slow, thus creating some suspense and also giving time to introduce some text, if necessary. However, while the movie is being played, the dissolves between clips can be shorter, in particular, when our intention is to create a sense of vivacity and a dynamic environment.

Camera effects

Chapter 8, Getting Realism with Camera Effects, was entirely dedicated to the camera effects that we can add to the images or movies we create in Lumion. The goal was to achieve realism using some camera effects in order to reproduce what happens in the real world. However, there is one special effect that we can add to our movie, and the final output will be simply striking, almost removing the CG look. Let's see how we can use and apply the **Handheld Camera** effect.

Getting ready

For the **Handheld Camera** effect, we need one clip in order to understand how the effect works.

How to do it...

To apply the **Handheld Camera** effect, perform the following steps:

1. Select the clip and click on the **New effect** button to add another effect to your clip.

2. In the **Movie effect** library, open the **Camera** tab and select the **Handheld Camera** effect.

3. The module added to the movie mode interface will look something like the following screenshot:

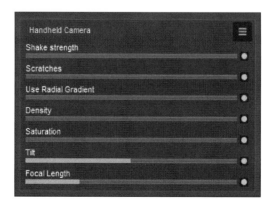

4. Play the clip with the default settings; you will not see any difference before and after you apply the effect.

5. The setting that controls the **Handheld Camera** effect directly is the **Shake strength** setting. By default, the value is **0**, and you need to increase this value to start seeing the effect in action.

6. Increase the **Shake strength** setting to a value between 1 and 1.5 if you want a subtle handheld effect.

7. If you play the clip again, the effect has now become more noticeable, and it produces a more natural look.

8. You don't need to stop here because the **Handheld Camera** effect gives you access to more settings to control the camera.

9. Using this effect, you can imitate a vintage camera using the **Scratches**, **Use Radial Gradient**, **Density**, and **Saturation** settings.

10. Set the **Scratches** value to **0.5** and this will add some vignette to your clip along with some scratches and other artifacts that were common in old recording cameras.

11. To help you find the best value for your scene, you can play the clip and start tweaking the settings and see it in real time to learn how the settings affect the image.

12. The **Use Radial Gradient**, **Density**, and **Saturation** settings work in conjunction.

13. The **Use Radial Gradient** setting will only start producing a blow out effect with values that are higher than **0.5**, and you can use a value of **0.3** for the **Density** and **Saturation** settings to control the strength of this effect.

14. The **Focal Length** setting is a familiar setting that is also available to you when you create a camera path, but another setting that can be used to create some interesting camera angles is the **Tilt** setting.

15. You can increase or decrease the value of the **Tilt** setting to rotate the camera.

Using the Titles effect

In some instances, it is necessary that we add text to explain a concept, introduce a material, or guide the viewer throughout the walk-through. In Lumion, we have an option to add text to the scene, but this always doesn't fulfill the requirements we have and it lacks diversity. However, it is possible to add text directly to a movie and control it using some remarkably simple settings. Let's see how we can use the **Titles** effect.

Getting ready

To apply this effect, we need at least one clip in the **Movie** mode.

How to do it...

To add text to your clip, perform the following steps:

1. After you select the clip, you need to add a new effect.

2. Click on the **New effect** button, and from the **Style** tab, select the **Titles** effect.

3. A module is added to the movie interface, as you can see in the following screenshot:

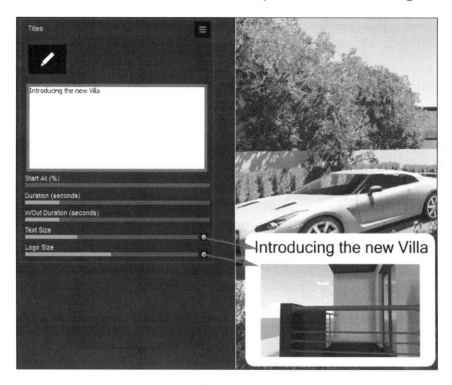

4. Start by typing the text in the white field, as you can see in the previous screenshot.

5. Then, change the **Start At (%)** setting to **10**. This means that if your clip is 30 seconds long, the text will appear after 3 seconds because you are using a value of 10 percent.

6. The **Duration (seconds)** and **In/Out Duration (seconds)** settings, on the other hand, are controlled by using seconds.

7. Adjust the **Text Size** and **Logo Size** settings to frame the text and the logo of your clip.

8. In the previous screenshot, there is already a logo and the text is on the bottom-left corner of the screen, which is different from what you may have on your screen. This is because when you add this effect, the settings available are just the tip of the iceberg.

9. Click on the button that is represented by the pencil icon; this will open a window where you have access to at least 27 styles of titles to be used, as you can see in the following screenshot:

10. You can say "at least 27 styles" because as you can see in the previous screenshot, it is possible to change the title's color and create a different transition using additional styles, when available.

11. Use the **Custom** button to use a specific font type for your title. With this, you can change the title's position using the menu on the left-hand side of the screen, as you can see in the screenshot.

12. Finally, it is possible to add a logo or an image that will be attached to the title, so this should not be confused with adding a logo to the entire movie because the logo image in this effect will appear and disappear with the title.

13. Click on the **OK** button to return to the **Movie** mode and save all the changes.

Framing and composition

Framing and composition are two fundamental aspects that help you transform a boring shot into something far more interesting. Throughout this Cookbook, the famous rule of thirds has been mentioned several times, but there is more skill involved in creating a well-balanced and pleasant shot. This recipe is going to help you understand some basic rules and show how you can create interesting shots.

Getting ready

For this recipe, we are going to see several good and not so good examples of how we can compose and frame a particular shot.

How to do it...

Let's start by opening the **Movie** mode and performing the following steps:

1. Select a blank clip and click on the **Record** button to start recording a camera path.

2. The first concept you need to keep in mind is that the center square is not always the best move, and the following screenshot shows an example of a shot where the centre square is used:

3. Instead of centering your shot on one object or person, try to use the four imaginary points that the grid creates. This will generally result in a pleasant and balanced composition, as you can see in the next screenshot:

4. Try to move the camera so that the person or object appears where two of the lines meet. This doesn't mean that they have to be right on the intersection, but close to it is good enough, and the same lines can help you keep the horizon level and the vertical elements in your shot straight.

5. This concept can create a more interesting photo, but it also leaves the scene with a feeling of emptiness, so you need to balance the weight of the shot by including other less important objects to fill some space.

6. The next screenshot shows a good example of where to place the horizon line; most pictures look better if the horizon is positioned above or below the middle of the frame:

7. The previous screenshot also shows you how you can use trees and other elements to create natural frames. This is called framing. Framing involves placing these elements, such as trees and mountains, around the edge of the composition to help you create a more focused image. Such images naturally draw the eye of the viewer to the main point of interest.

There's more...

We are not limited to just those few points mentioned in the recipe. We can use or break symmetry and patterns to create eye-catching compositions. The viewpoint is also important because it has a massive impact on the composition. So, instead of creating a movie using just the eye level, we can consider using a high or low level and even a close up.

Adding sound

An additional way to enhance the movie we are creating is by using an essential element called sound. Lumion give us the freedom to add sound and create a nice environment, as well as import an audio file to use in our movie. There are different features available, and this recipe is going to help you understand the differences between the features and how to make the best of these features.

Getting ready

For the first half of the recipe, we are going to need a clip in the **Movie** mode, and for second half, we just need a simple scene.

How to do it...

Let's start by adding the **Sound** effect; this can be done by performing the following steps:

1. Open the **Movie** mode and click on the **Entire Movie** button because the **Sound** effect only works in this mode, and you cannot apply it to individual clips.

2. Click on the **New effect** button to open the **Movie effect** library.

3. Open the **Objects** tab and select the **Sound** effect; by doing this, a module is added to your movie interface, as shown in the next screenshot:

4. This effect lets you choose an audio file that needs to be in the WAV format; use this as the background sound.

5. To control the volume of the sound, adjust the **Music** setting because the **SFX** setting is used to control the sounds that you place in your project.

6. One thing you need to keep in mind is that you need an audio file with the same length of the movie; otherwise, the sound will be repeated.

7. The second option to add sound is by placing this element in the scene using the **Build** mode.

8. Go to the **Build** mode and from the left-hand side of the screen, select the **Objects** menu.

9. In this menu, click on the **Sound** button to open the **Sound Library** window, as shown in the following screenshot:

10. Place the mouse over any thumbnail and a sound preview starts to play. Click on a thumbnail to select the sound and place this sound in the scene, like you do to place other objects.

11. The sound clip immediately starts to play, but if you start to move away, the sound starts to fade and eventually the clip stops playing.

12. You can edit sound properties by selecting the **Edit properties** option and clicking on the sound to open the **Sound Properties** window, as you can see in the following screenshot:

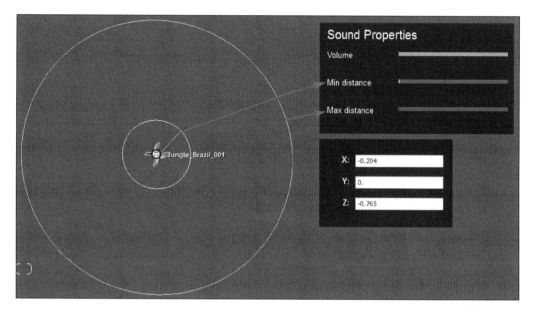

13. As highlighted in the previous screenshot, the controls for this element are quite simple. The green circle, the **Max distance** setting, represents where the sound starts to become noticeable; when the camera approaches the yellow circle, that is, the **Min distance** setting, the sound will be at full volume.

14. You can change these values and see the video in real time to learn about the influence that sound will have once you adjust the settings.

15. After this, you can move the camera to the green circle and see whether you need to make any further adjustments.

12
Rendering

In this chapter, we will cover the following recipes:

- Exporting videos
- Rendering individual clips
- Rendering stills
- Rendering an image sequence
- Broadcasting on TV
- Working with perspectives
- Rendering passes

Introduction

Throughout this Cookbook, we have been learning about methods and best practices to produce gorgeous still images and using Lumion's camera effects to achieve a certain level of realism. Moreover, in *Chapter 10, Bringing Your World to Life*, and *Chapter 11, Creating Videos*, we learned how to use animation tools to create and manage clips with special features. So, now it is the time to export these clips and transform them into a movie.

This chapter is essentially an overview of the process for exporting a video; however, we will also cover different techniques to export single clips and create a sequence of images that can be used later in applications such as Adobe After Effects and Premiere. Also, we will cover two special features that will help us export a video to be broadcasted on TV and other practical applications of working with perspectives.

Exporting videos

Now it's time to export our amazing clips and convert them into a movie that can be sent to the client or even broadcasted on TV. This recipe is simple to follow, but there are some characteristics that we need to take into consideration before exporting the movie. We will not only learn how to export a movie, but also form some guidelines to improve the rendering time.

Getting ready

For this recipe, we at least need a clip that uses the recording option or other two options such as importing an image or an external video file.

How to do it...

To export a video, perform the following steps:

1. Start by opening the **Movie** mode.

2. With this mode open, create a clip if you don't have any clip present in your project.

3. While creating the clips, you can verify the reflections and lights that are used by pressing the *U* key. This feature shows the reflections and lights in full quality and helps you check whether you need to make any further adjustments.

4. To export the clips as a movie, click on the **Save Movie** button, as you can see in the following screenshot:

5. This action opens a window that allows you to export the movie straightaway without any additional configurations; the settings used by default export a movie with **30** frames per second that is of the best quality and a resolution of **720p**.

6. Click on the **Auto** button to have access to more settings, as shown in the next screenshot:

7. To know what each setting provides, place your mouse over each value and a small description will appear.

8. In most circumstances, you will want full quality; however, if you need to send an initial draft to a client to verify the animation and other elements, you can use the lowest quality from the **Final output quality** setting.

9. After choosing the settings that are adequate to your project, click on the **Start movie export** button to select the folder where you want to save the MP4 file.

10. A new interface appears that shows the video is being rendered, and you have an option to pause or stop the rendering process by pressing the *Esc* key.

11. When Lumion finishes rendering the video, it will go back to the **Movie** mode.

How it works...

We can work on different tasks while Lumion is rendering the movie. This is possible because Lumion always renders movies in the background; however, it is recommended that you wait until the first image is rendered before switching to a different application.

The render time for our movie will depend not only on our workstation's specifications, such as the graphic card, but it also depends on the complexity of our project. This means that if you add more 3D models and objects from the Lumion library, it will increase the complexity of the project. So, we can use layers and the several layer effects to hide 3D models that are not viewed by the camera.

Rendering individual clips

Lumion allows us not only to export an entire movie, but it also gives us the autonomy to render or export individual clips. Every time we click on the **Save Movie** button, the entire movie is exported. So, this opportunity of exporting single clips can be quite useful, in particular, when we wish to manipulate these different clips later with video editing applications such as Adobe Premiere. Let's see how we can export one clip at a time.

Getting ready

For this recipe, we need to create one simple clip to understand how this feature works.

How to do it...

To render an individual clip, perform the following steps:

1. After you open the **Movie** mode, select a clip you wish to export.

2. Once selected, two buttons will appear over the clip, as shown in the following screenshot:

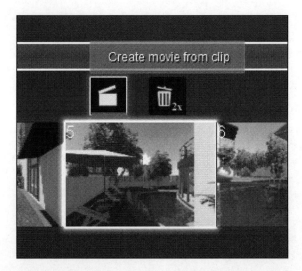

3. The button with the trash bin icon lets you delete the clip, but be careful because there is no undo option for this action. You need to double-click on this button to delete the clip.

4. Select the **Create movie from clip** button; this will give you access to the same export options that you get when you export an entire movie.

5. Once you have finished rendering, you need to select another clip and repeat the fourth step.

6. This means that if you have five clips, you need to perform this step every single time in order to export all five clips.

How it works...

To reduce the time it takes to render individual clips, we may want to check the use of lights with dynamic shadows and make sure that lights which are at a certain distance from the camera use either the **Memory** or **Speed** options that can be found in the **Light Properties** menu.

Another tip is to restart Lumion before starting the rendering process because this action of rendering complex scenes can improve the time it takes to render as well. Finally, if we are exporting just a draft, we can navigate to the **Settings** menu and switch on the **Limit all texture sizes 512x512 and save a bit of memory for huge scenes or low end graphics cards** option.

Rendering stills

The **Photo** mode is where we can export still images, and this mode will be our first option when we need to export some images. However, it is possible to perform almost the same action and export single images using the **Movie** mode. This recipe is going to help us understand how we can do that and why we should think about the **Movie** mode as an alternative to the **Photo** mode.

Getting ready

For this recipe, we need to record a clip and create an interesting camera path with some key camera angles, because we will be using this to export our images.

How to do it...

To render still images, perform the following steps:

1. Open the **Movie** mode and select the clip that you wish to use to export single images.

2. Before exporting your image, and because you are using a clip, you have to specify which frame of the clip has to be exported.

3. Using the clip bar or the scrubbing feature, go back and forth in time until you find the perfect camera angle that you want to use to export the image.

4. On the right-hand side of the screen, click on the **Save Movie** button to open the window, where you can get access to the options to export a video file.

5. At the top of the window, you will find three tabs: one to export an MP4 file, second to export images, and third to export a single image, as shown in the following screenshot:

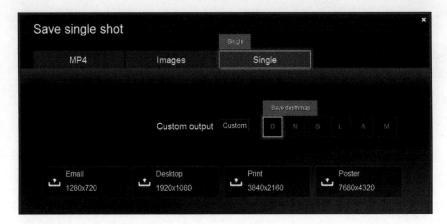

6. To export an image, you need to choose one of the four resolutions available; this will open a new window where you can choose the folder to save the image.

7. Look back at the previous screenshot and click on the **Auto** button to access a few more preferences and click on the first letter to save a depthmap.

8. Again, select a resolution or the image size and select the folder where you want to save the image.

9. Check the rendered image and you will see that this image has nothing to do with the one saved previously.

10. This happens because you activated the **Custom output** option, where you can save up to six different types and formats that can later be used to improve the look of an image.

11. In order to save a normal image again, you need to click on the **Custom** button to deactivate the custom output.

How it works...

When we select the **Custom output** option, we are, in reality, getting an element that composes our image because when those six different elements are combined together, we get a colored image.

However, we can export this colored image and use these individual elements to correct or improve some areas in the image. So, this option has some advantages over the traditional method of exporting just the colored image, giving us more control over the final output when using an external application such as Adobe Photoshop or Gimp.

> ▶ To learn what each render pass does, check the *Using special formats* recipe in *Chapter 9, Non-photorealistic Effects*

Rendering an image sequence

A movie is made up of a sequence of frames that we play at a high speed, and this gives us the impression that a car is moving or a person is walking. However, instead of exporting a video file, we can export the movie as a sequence of images. Once more, this feature is useful when we do some post-production work with an external application. Let's see how we can export an image sequence and a set of images.

Getting ready

For this recipe, we need to record a clip using five or any other number of snapshots because we will be using this to export our images using a singular feature.

How to do it...

To export an image sequence, perform the following steps:

1. In the **Movie** mode, after creating at least one clip, click on the **Save Movie** button.

2. By default, Lumion shows you the **MP4** tab to export a video file, but for this recipe, select the second tab called **Images**.

3. You need to click on the **Auto** button to access more settings and control the type of output you need for your project.

4. The first three options, namely, **Frames per second**, **Final output quality**, and **Choose resolution**, are the same that you find when exporting a movie.

5. The **Custom output** option, as mentioned in the previous recipe, lets you export several specific elements, such as lighting, reflections, and other formats that can be later combined with your original image, thus giving you more control over the final output.

6. The next setting is where you can find some useful features to export an image sequence and much more.

7. Under the **Frame range** setting, you need to select the **Range** option. So, if the **Shots** option is available, click on it once to access the **Range** option.

8. With the **Range** option, you have two text fields with some numbers inside, as shown in the following screenshot:

9. As you can see in the previous screenshot, the two fields have the values **0** and **3558**, and by default, the values will be the first and the last frame of the movie, giving you the full extent of the movie.

10. If you place the mouse over one of these fields, a small preview will appear, as shown in the previous screenshot, and this will help you verify the frame you selected.

11. Click on the **OK** button to save the sequence of images in a folder, and the render process will begin and depend on your project.

12. It is important that you select the correct **frames per second** (**FPS**) because this will influence the amount of images that are exported. Then, when importing the images on another application, you need to specify what FPS you have used.

13. The next feature is very useful to quickly export a set of images of your movie. To have a smoother workflow, Lumion has a nice feature that you can find in the **Frame range** setting.

14. Click on the **Range** option to change for **Shot**, and if you have created a clip using five snapshots or any other number, you will notice that when you use this option to export the images, Lumion will read the snapshots you used to create the clip and export them.

15. Click on the **OK** button and Lumion will start rendering all the snapshots you used to create all the clips present in your scene.

How it works...

Keep in mind that if you use any additional custom outputs, let's say **Depthmap** and **Material ID**, Lumion will render the colored image first and then it will render these two additional formats; this will be done for every single frame.

Broadcasting on TV

National Television Standards Committee (**NTSC**) and **Phase Alternating Line** (**PAL**) are formats for videos. The differences between these two formats are the reason why some DVDs from Europe may not play in Japan and in other countries as well. Most of the times, this is not a big issue, because the video we send to the client will be played on a computer or uploaded on the Internet; however, it is good to know that Lumion provides us with this possibility to create a movie using either the NTSC or PAL format. Let's see how we can do that.

Getting ready

We need a simple clip in order to apply the effects and see the differences between each format.

How to do it...

To add the PAL or NTSC option to the video file, perform the following steps:

1. Open the **Movie** mode and click on the **New effect** button to open the **Movie effect** library.

2. In the **Artistic** tab, you can find the **Broadcast safe** effect.

3. Select this effect and you will notice that the effect is applied not to your clip, but to the entire movie.

4. The effect is simple with only two buttons, as you can see in the following screenshot:

5. Select either the **Pal** or **Ntsc** option and you can be assured that your movie will be safely played at the final destination.

6. You need to be aware that this is also another difference between these two formats. When exporting a movie using NTSC, select a **Frames per second** value of **30**; if it is the PAL format, you need to use **25** FPS.

There's more...

The countries that use the PAL system are North America, Japan, and South Korea, and the NTSC system is used in most of Europe, Australia, and large parts of Asia and Africa.

Working with perspectives

A perspective is a way of drawing objects in 3D, and Lumion uses the 3-point perspective. We can however apply an effect to get a 2-point perspective, where we use two vanishing points to create an image or a clip ensuring that the vertical lines remain vertical no matter what the camera angle is. This can be used to create technical and conceptual illustrations, and this recipe is going to teach us how we can use one effect in Lumion to achieve the same result.

Getting ready

The effect we are going to use in this recipe can be applied to both images and clips, but for this recipe, we will apply the effect to a clip.

How to do it...

To work with the **2-Point Perspective** effect, perform the following steps:

1. Create a clip in the **Movie** mode.

2. Using the **New effect** button, open the **Movie effect** library.

3. Go to the **Camera** tab and locate the **2-Point Perspective** effect. Select it to add this effect to your clip. The following screenshot shows you an example of a clip without the effect applied. Notice how the vertical lines are not vertical:

4. Initially, there is no change in your clip, and this is because you need to turn this effect on. Drag the slider to a value of around **0.5** to switch this effect on and see the immediate result, as shown in the following screenshot:

5. You may need to adjust the camera slightly to encompass the entire building. Double-click on the clip to edit and rearrange the camera.

There's more...

One good use of the **2-Point Perspective** effect is the opportunity to easily achieve straight vertical lines without losing time. Then, we can use other artistic effects to reproduce watercolor visualizations or some technical illustrations for facades.

Rendering passes

Rendering passes is the process of rendering different attributes of our scene separately and composing them together to produce the final output that is rendered. Some of the elements available in Lumion are Specular, Lighting, Depth of Field, and some special elements such as Material ID and Skyalpha. We can extract these elements and put everything together in most post-production software that supports the compositing of layers, thereby giving us much greater control over the look of the final result. Let's see how we can access and use these rendering passes.

Getting ready

For this recipe, we can create a small clip using only one snapshot in order to have an image to export. To see how **Material ID** and **Depthmap** work, it will be good to add some 3D models to our scene.

How to do it...

Let's start by opening the **Movie** mode and performing the following steps:

1. Select a clip and click on the **Save Movie** button to access the option to export several special formats.

2. Select the second tab called **Images**, and in the **Custom output** setting, click on the **Auto** button to access the custom options.

3. Here, you can find six buttons that represent six different special formats or render passes, as shown in the following screenshot:

4. You need to click on one of the buttons in order to select the render pass that will be exported when you save the movie.

5. One of the advantages of using this feature is the opportunity to export all the render passes in one go. This is different from the **Single** option, where you can only save one render pass at a time.

6. Click on the **OK** button to save and export the sequence of images.

See also

▸ To learn what each render pass does, check the *Using special formats* recipe in *Chapter 9, Non-photorealistic Effects*

13
Lighting

In this chapter, we will cover the following recipes:

- ▸ Using spotlights
- ▸ Previewing spotlights
- ▸ Configuring the properties of light
- ▸ Setting up shadows
- ▸ Tweaking the Global Illumination effect
- ▸ Using the Exposure effect
- ▸ Working with reflection control

Introduction

The real-time technology that powers Lumion provides us with a very believable and reliable lighting solution, and this is one of the key features to create the most beautiful still images and movies. Throughout this Cookbook, we learned many recipes that covered how to use the **Weather** system. This includes tools to control natural elements and also some significant effects that can be applied to have a more accurate control over the sun, clouds, and other features that contribute towards developing a good mood and lighting. Most of these features focus on exterior scenes, and they are fantastic; nonetheless, Lumion being a very powerful tool has a set of tools and lights that can be used for interior and nighttime scenes as well. In this chapter, we will cover how we can use these lights and tweak other features to create the perfect interior renders.

Using spotlights

One category of lights that can be found in Lumion is the spotlight. Lumion's spotlight is a very versatile light, and with this light, we can reproduce practically every source of light found in the real world. This recipe is going to introduce us to spotlights and some will provide us with tips to use this light.

Getting ready

For this recipe, we need to create a nighttime scene, so we don't have any influence from the sun over the interior lighting that we will add to the scene. To create a night scene, select the **Weather** menu, and from this menu, use the **Sun height** setting to transform a day scene into a night scene.

How to do it...

To add a spotlight to your scene, perform the following steps:

1. You can create a layer called `Lights_Interior` and use this layer to organize all the lights you have in the interior of the building, and if needed, create a second layer for exterior lights.

2. From the left-hand side of the screen, select the **Objects** menu and click on the **Lights and special objects** button.

3. Click on the **Change object** button to open the **Lights and Utilities Library** window.

4. Select the first tab called **Light**; here, you can find 30 types of spotlights. Each thumbnail is a demonstration of the IES profile that shows how the light will appear when placed in a scene. The effect shown by a thumbnail is perceived more when the light is close to the surfaces.

5. Select a spotlight and you'll be back to the **Build** mode controlling a yellow boundary box that represents the light.

6. Click on it with the left mouse button to place the light, and you will see that the wireframe of the spotlight becomes visible showing you the cone of the light that is produced. Keep the mouse button pressed and drag the cone of the light up and down to adjust the height.

7. You can use the most common tools such as the move, rotate, and scale tools to control the location of the light.

There's more...

When placing these lights in our scene, it is worthy enough to remember that the amount of light present in the scene will affect the render time. In order to create an optimized scene, we need to carefully plan the amount of light that is required and the quality of the shadow. It is usually a good idea to place the spotlights with good shadow accuracy closer to the camera or the 3D models. The light and the shadows will be much better, and this is something that is needed for 3D models which are close to the camera. Then, we can use some more economic spotlights, with the memory setting selected, to fill the scene with extra light.

Previewing spotlights

Being a real-time engine, Lumion's main goal is to provide the best performance possible while building and creating the 3D world. Spotlights and other lights can be very memory consuming, so Lumion tries to balance this between shadow accuracy and optimization by showing a preview of the light and not its full quality. This recipe is going to cover a very simple way to see a light in full quality and also how we can use other lights to balance the use of spotlights.

Getting ready

Like with the previous recipe, we need a nighttime scene to see the full effect of lights in the scene. To create a night scene, select the **Weather** menu, and using the **Sun height** setting, transform the day scene into a night scene. When creating the night scene, Lumion's camera will take a few seconds to adjust to this environment with low light.

How to do it...

Let's start by adding lights to your scene; for this, perform the following steps:

1. From the left-hand side of the screen, select the **Objects** menu and click on the **Lights and special objects** button.

2. Click on the **Change object** button to open the **Lights and Utilities Library** window.

3. Select a spotlight and start populating your project with a few lights; notice how every time you place a light, you will be able to see the shadows that are produced by that light.

4. Even with full quality enabled, your scene looks a little bit dull and flat. This is because of the absence of shadows. This is a process that Lumion uses to save some memory while you are working in the **Build** mode.

5. To see the light with shadows, you need to do something as simple as select the light or lights. The quickest way of doing this is by pressing the *Ctrl* key, and with the left mouse button, clicking-and-dragging it to draw a rectangle selection around the light or lights according to your needs. This action will show you the shadows, as you can see in the following screenshot:

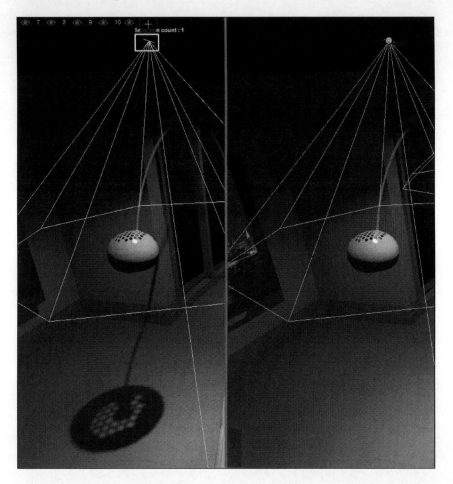

6. The second way to select a light is by using the **Context** menu that becomes available when you place the spotlights. Back in the **Objects** menu, click on the **Context** menu and select the light.

7. A submenu appears with two options; click on the **Selection...** option and a range of new options becomes available. At this stage, you can decide whether you want to select an individual light by using the **Select** option or select all the lights in the scene using the **Select All Similar** option.

8. Use the **Select All Similar** option to select all the lights in your scene and have a look at the shadows produced by the lights in your scene.

9. After checking the scene, you may feel tempted to add a few more spotlights to light some dark corners or not-so-well-lit areas. Lumion has another light that can be used in these situations called **light fill**, and this will help you save valuable memory resources.

10. Again, select the **Objects** menu and click on the **Lights and special objects** button.

11. Click on the **Change object** button to open the **Lights and Utilities Library** window and then click on the **Light** tab. With this, you will be able to see two small squares that represent the number of additional tabs.

12. Select the second square; at this point, you will find only three lights. Click on **light fill**, the third one, to place this light in your scene.

13. Click on the scene with the left mouse button to place this light, but try to place the light in the middle of your scene as this light is to fill the environment.

14. Immediately, you can see how the scene becomes much brighter without having to use additional spotlights.

How it works...

The **light fill** option works like an ambient light, and it helps to save memory resources by removing the need to use extra spotlights to light the scene. Plus, the **light fill** option will not produce any shadows, so we can use more than one light fill to light different areas of our scene.

Configuring the properties of light

The control we have over the lights placed in our scene is amplified and taken to the next level with the use of the **Edit properties** menu. Lumion's light that offers more control is the spotlight, and this recipe is going to cover how we can tweak this light, use some techniques to improve our workflow, and improve the efficiency when lighting interior scenes.

Getting ready

If you are following the previous recipes, you should have now a nighttime scene with some spotlights and light fill placed. We are going to use these lights to explain how we can configure the light properties.

How to do it...

To configure the light properties, perform the following steps:

1. To configure the properties of a spotlight or any other light, you need to ensure that the **Objects** menu is open and the **Lights and special objects** button selected.

2. After following the previous step, locate and select the **Edit properties** button, which is shown in the following screenshot:

3. The next step is to select the light or multiple lights by pressing the *Ctrl* key, and with the left mouse button, clicking-and-dragging it to draw a selection rectangle. When you select a light, the **Light Properties** window appears, which is shown in the following screenshot:

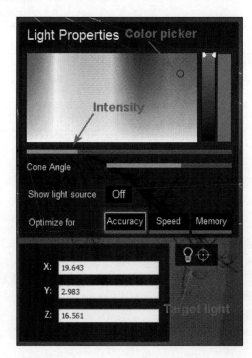

4. Use the **color picker** marker to select a new color for the light emitted from the spotlight. The color is important to set the mood for the scene. For example, a living room with a fireplace will benefit if you use the lights with an orange or reddish color, suggesting a warm environment.

5. The next step is to set the intensity of the light and for that you need to adjust the **Overbright** slider below the **color picker** marker. If you feel that the scene needs extra illumination, it is a good idea to leave this adjustment for when your scene is completed with all the lights. This will help you to see whether there is a need to increase or decrease the intensity of the light.

6. The **Cone Angle** setting is useful to change the area that the spotlight covers with light. Using the highest value possible on this setting can be useful when you need to light big environments, but this will create softer shadows with lesser detail.

7. If you are using this spotlight to mimic a light source such as a lamp in the ceiling, use the **Show light source** option. Lumion will add an overbright spot to the spotlight, but when using a light with low intensity, this will result in the creation of a small circle that will not look good when the lamp is bigger.

8. In order to achieve a better result, increase the value of the **Overbright** slider. You can balance the intensity of the light by adjusting the color's intensity or by using the **Exposure** effect.

9. To improve the render time, you need to pay close attention to the next setting called **Optimize for**. The **Accuracy** setting creates shadows that are dynamic and of good quality but increases the render time. The **Memory** setting is good to improve the render time, but the shadow quality is very low.

10. The final feature that can be used to help light your scene is the **Target light(s)** setting. Click on this button, and then using the left mouse button, click-and-drag it to a target where the spotlight or several spotlights are pointing to. To finish lighting your scene, click on the **Back** button to save the final position.

How it works...

To aid the decision of what settings we need to use in our scene, we have to strike a balance between good shadow quality and render time; the following is a small explanation about each setting.

Let's start with the **Accuracy** setting. The shadows created by the spotlight are updated in every frame, so if an object is moving, the shadow will also move, and this will increase the render time. This also means that every time we add a light with **Accuracy** turned on, it is another shadow that needs to be calculated for every frame. With this setting, use a 2048 x 2048 pixel shadow texture, which provides a very accurate and detailed shadow.

The **Speed** setting provides the best of both the worlds because it doesn't increase the render time much, and the shadow quality is acceptable because it only uses a static 512 x 512 pixel texture; also, the shadow is not calculated for every frame. Finally, the **Memory** setting is the setting that probably doesn't increase the render time at all because it only uses a static 128 x 128 pixel texture, which is not updated. These last two options have one important detail, and the next screenshot shows the lighting that is done with spotlights using the **Speed** and **Memory** settings:

Because we used a spotlight with the **Speed** or **Memory** settings, if we move the object after the light is being placed, the shadow will remain and won't be updated; the reason for this is that both **Speed** and **Memory** use static shadows. This should pose a problem for a scene where we have static objects, but if we have any objects moving around, we need to use spotlights with the **Accuracy** setting. To update the shadow, we need to click, for example, on the **Accuracy** button and select the **Speed** or **Memory** setting again.

Setting up shadows

Placing lights is just half of the work, and we need to achieve an attractive and believable interior lighting. The next step is to control what those lights will produce, which will be shadows. In the previous recipes, we learned how we can preview the shadow produced by the spotlight and also the different shadow qualities that are available, but this recipe is going to teach you how to tweak the shadows using the **Shadow** effect.

Getting ready

For this recipe, we need a nighttime scene with some spotlights present.

How to do it...

To set up the spotlight's shadows, perform the following steps:

1. Open the **Photo** mode and place the camera in a position where you can see the spotlight and its shadow that is formed.

2. In the **Photo** mode, to see the shadow produced by the spotlight, you need to add the **Global Illumination** effect.

3. Click on the **New effect** button, and from the **World** tab, select the **Global Illumination** effect.

4. Keep the default settings for the **Global Illumination** effect because the shadows are now visible and our goal is to add a second effect to control them.

5. Click on the **New effect** button, and from the **World** tab, select the **Shadow** effect.

6. When working with interior lighting, the shadows play a big role in turning the scene into something pleasing. To control and improve the shadows created by the spotlights in the scene, adjust the **Brightness** value.

7. When working with interior illumination, it is normal to have some shadows in the corners and areas where the walls touch other geometrical structures. The **Brightness** slider helps to remove some of these shadows. When increasing this setting, you could end up with colored shadows, and to balance them, use the **Coloring** setting.

8. Next, you need to start tweaking the **Ambient scale**, **Ambient**, and **Ambient diffuse** settings to clean the scene from any contact shadows, but don't remove these shadows entirely because they also help in producing a more believable image or movie.

How it works...

When creating interior scenes, and in particular with nighttime illumination, Lumion needs some adjustments to improve not only the interior lighting, but also the shadows produced by these lights. Using the **Shadows** effect will help us strike a balance between good lighting and removing any blotchiness from the shadows. Using the **light fill** option in these situations can also improve the final look of our still image or movie.

Tweaking the Global Illumination effect

When working with interior scenes, we may have a good proportion of light that comes from the windows in the room or other areas in the building; however, the light is not reflected back to the ceiling and other elements in the scene. Lumion has an effect that can help us add more light to our scene without using additional lights. Let's see how we can use the **Global Illumination** effect with interior renders.

Getting ready

To follow this recipe, we need an interior scene with some windows and at least one spotlight. For the first half of the recipe, we will use a daytime scene and then change it to a nighttime scene. We are going to use the **Photo** mode to exemplify the effects, but the same principles and effects can be used with the **Movie** mode.

How to do it...

To control and bring more light to the interior scene, perform the following steps:

1. Open the **Photo** mode and place the camera in a good position to see the full extent of your scene.

2. Click on the **New effect** button to open the **Photo effect** library.

3. Under the **World** tab, locate and select the **Global Illumination** effect.

4. If you are working on a daytime scene, start by increasing the **Sun amount** slider; this action makes the sunlight bounce around the environment, bringing more light to the scene.

5. You can check the result of this effect by clicking on and then switching off the **Preview Spotlight GI and Shadows** button.

6. For a daytime scene, the use of this effect will be enough to have a well-lit room with plenty of sunlight, but things change when you work with a nighttime scene.

7. Change the scene from daytime to nighttime and you will see that the **Sun amount** setting has no effect on the scene. Now, it is time to realize that the spotlights in your scene can make all the difference.

8. Click on the **Select lights** button, as shown in the following screenshot:

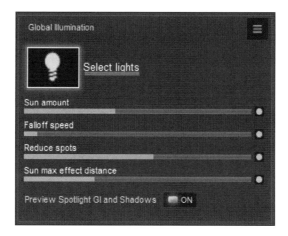

9. Click on this button and the **Build** mode appears, but the only options you have are to select the lights and control the amount of GI produced by spotlights, as you can see in the following screenshot:

10. With the left mouse button, click on the options to select the spotlights you want to control with this feature; then, using the **Spotlight GI amount** slider, start to adjust the spotlight's influence over the scene and the light that is produced.

11. When you are happy with the result, click on the **Back** button to save the changes, and if necessary, use the **Reduce spots** setting to remove any lighting artifact that might be present in the scene.

How it works...

When working with the **Spotlight GI** feature, we don't need to select all the spotlights present in the scene. Start by selecting the key lights in the scene and adjust the **Spotlight GI amount** setting. If necessary, select secondary lights; however, usually two or three lights are enough to bring extra light into the scene.

Using the Exposure effect

Exposure is the amount of light captured by the sensor in a real camera during a single picture. If the shot is exposed for too long, the image will be washed out or too bright, but on the other hand, if the shot is exposed for a shorter period of time, the image will be too dark. Lumion lets you do the same thing using an effect called **Exposure**. This can be especially useful when working with interior lighting with spotlights where it is more likely to have issues with overbright areas.

Getting ready

For this recipe, we need an interior scene with some spotlights present, and we can increase the intensity or the **Overbright** setting in order to have an overbright scene.

How to do it...

After placing and tweaking the spotlights in your project, perform the following steps to use the **Exposure** effect:

1. From the **Photo** mode, select the **New effect** button.

2. Inside the **Photo effect** library, you can find the **Exposure** effect under the **Camera** tab.

3. Click on the **Exposure** effect and a new module will be added to your scene, as shown in the following screenshot:

4. By default, the value used is **0.5**, and this means that there is no change in the scene.

5. If your scene is too dark, you can increase the **Exposure** value; alternatively, if the scene is too bright, you can decrease the **Exposure** value to darken the image.

6. You may need to keyframe the values used, in particular, when you have an animation that goes from an exterior to an interior environment and vice versa.

How it works...

When lighting an interior scene, sometimes we find out that having a balanced lighting and gloom through the light sources is not possible. The workaround is to increase the **Overbright** value until the gloom and brightness is perceptible in the light source, but you end up with a scene that is overexposed. The solution is to use the **Exposure** effect in order to eliminate any extra amount of brightness. Suppose you have an animation that goes from an exterior to an interior environment and the exposure used needs to be adjusted so we don't have a very dark interior area. Once again, in such scenarios, the **Exposure** effect can give us a hand, and using keyframes, it is possible to create an enjoyable transition.

Working with reflection control

An additional possibility to improve the reflections in our renders is the use of a **reflection control** object. This is the easiest way to add more accurate reflections to the glass surfaces and other elements that produce reflectivity. This proves specially useful when creating interior lighting, and because we are already making good use of spotlights, the use of a **reflection control** object can provide an extra touch to our renders without increasing the render time. Let's see how we can use the **reflection control** object in Lumion.

Getting ready

In order to fully understand and see the effect of the **reflection control** object, we need a scene with reflective surfaces, in particular, windows where it will be easier to see the results.

How to do it...

To add a **reflection control** object to your project, perform the following steps:

1. In the **Build** mode, open the **Objects** menu that is found on the left-hand side of the screen.

2. Click on the **Lights and special objects** button and then click on the **Change object** button to open the **Lights And Utilities Library** window.

3. Open the third tab called **Utilities** and select the **reflection control** object, as shown in the following screenshot:

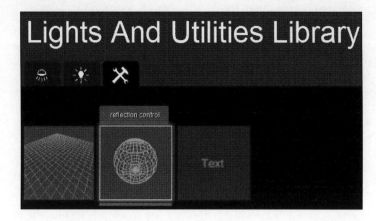

4. When you select this object, you are directed back to the **Build** mode, and now, you need to place this **reflection control** object somewhere in your scene.

5. With the left mouse button, click on the scene to place the **reflection control** object; after this, you can use the normal tools to control this object.

6. Immediately, you will see how this affects the glass and other elements in your scene. The position and the height of the **reflection control** object can make all the difference, and in reality, produce different results.

How it works...

Reflections in Lumion depend on a panoramic reflection texture that is projected onto all reflective materials, and by specifying the position of the **reflection control** object, we dictate where the panoramic reflection texture should be rendered. We can use the combination of *Ctrl + U* to update the reflection texture produced by this reflection control.

Index

About Packt Publishing

Packt, pronounced 'packed', published its first book "*Mastering phpMyAdmin for Effective MySQL Management*" in April 2004 and subsequently continued to specialize in publishing highly focused books on specific technologies and solutions.

Our books and publications share the experiences of your fellow IT professionals in adapting and customizing today's systems, applications, and frameworks. Our solution based books give you the knowledge and power to customize the software and technologies you're using to get the job done. Packt books are more specific and less general than the IT books you have seen in the past. Our unique business model allows us to bring you more focused information, giving you more of what you need to know, and less of what you don't.

Packt is a modern, yet unique publishing company, which focuses on producing quality, cutting-edge books for communities of developers, administrators, and newbies alike. For more information, please visit our website: www.packtpub.com.

Writing for Packt

We welcome all inquiries from people who are interested in authoring. Book proposals should be sent to author@packtpub.com. If your book idea is still at an early stage and you would like to discuss it first before writing a formal book proposal, contact us; one of our commissioning editors will get in touch with you.

We're not just looking for published authors; if you have strong technical skills but no writing experience, our experienced editors can help you develop a writing career, or simply get some additional reward for your expertise.

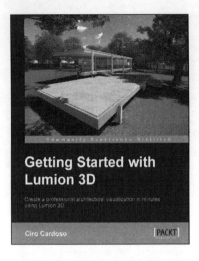

Getting Started with Lumion 3D

ISBN: 978-1-84969-949-5   Paperback: 134 pages

Create a professional architectural visualization in minutes using Lumion 3D

1. A beginner's guide to architectural visualization.

2. Tips and tricks for modeling, texturing, and rendering using Lumion 3D.

3. Add a special touch to your images with Photoshop.

KeyShot 3D Rendering

ISBN: 978-1-84969-482-7   Paperback: 124 pages

Showcase your 3D models and create hyperrealistic images with KeyShot in the fastest and most efficient way possible

1. Create professional quality images from your 3D models in just a few steps.

2. Thorough overview of how to work and navigate in KeyShot.

3. A step-by-step guide that quickly gets you started with creating realistic images.

Please check **www.PacktPub.com** for information on our titles

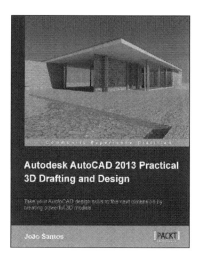

Autodesk AutoCAD 2013 Practical 3D Drafting and Design

ISBN: 978-1-84969-935-8   Paperback: 374 pages

Take your AutoCAD design skills to the next dimension by creating powerful 3D models

1. Obtain 2D drawings from 3D models.

2. Master AutoCAD's third dimension.

3. Full of practical tips and examples to help take your skills to the next dimension.

Google SketchUp for Game Design Beginner's Guide

ISBN: 978-1-84969-134-5   Paperback: 270 pages

Create 3D game worlds complete with textures, levels, and props

1. Learn how to create realistic game worlds with Google's easy 3D modeling tool.

2. Populate your games with realistic terrain, buildings, vehicles, and objects.

3. Import to game engines such as Unity 3D and create a first person 3D game simulation.

4. Learn the skills you need to sell low polygon 3D objects in game asset stores.

Please check **www.PacktPub.com** for information on our titles

12416444R00138

Printed in Great Britain
by Amazon